Missionaries, Mercenaries and Misfits

An anthology

Edited by
Rasna Warah

i

AuthorHouse™ UK Ltd.
500 Avebury Boulevard
Central Milton Keynes, MK9 2BE
www.authorhouse.co.uk
Phone: 08001974150

First published by AuthorHouse 7/14/2008

ISBN: 978-1-4343-8603-8 (sc)

Printed in the United Kingdom
Milton Keynes, England

This book is printed on acid-free paper.

Cover image by Xavier Verhoest.
Design by Michael Jones Software.

authorHOUSE®

Acknowledgements

On behalf of the publisher, I would like to thank the following copyright holders for permission to reproduce their work in this anthology:

Harper's magazine for "Journey to Nowhere" by Victoria Schlesinger, which was published under the title "The Continuation of Poverty" in its May 2007 edition; Bantu Mwaura for "Dancing to the Donor's Tune"; Parselelo Kantai for "The Maasai Invasions", which is adapted from an academic paper titled "In the Grip of the Vampire State: Maasai Land Struggles in Kenyan Politics" that appeared in the *Journal of East African Studies* (Vol. 1. No. 1, March 2007) published by Routledge Publishing, an imprint of Taylor and Francis; Kalundi Serumaga for "Unsettled"; the *Mail and Guardian* (South Africa) for "The Power of Love" by Binyavanga Wainaina; Isisaeli Kazado for "UN Blues" (The views expressed in this article are those of the author and do not necessarily reflect those of the United Nations); *Radical Philosophy* (www.radicalphilosophy.com) for "A Charitable Apartheid" by Lara Pawson, which was published in issue No. 131 (May/June 2005) under the title "You Let Her Into the House?"(The views expressed in this article are those of the author and do not necessarily reflect those of the BBC); Achal Prabhala for "The Activistocracy"; Onyango Oloo for "A Capitalist Carnival"; *The East African* for "The Good House Negro" by Philip Ochieng, which is adapted from an article titled "Abject Intellectual Surrender" that was published in its 28 April-4 May 2008 edition; Sunny Bindra for "Men Behaving Badly"; Maina Mwangi for "Why Aid Has Failed Africa So Spectacularly", which is based on a First Africa SA (Pty) Ltd. discussion paper presented at the 8th African Stock Exchanges Association Conference on 26 November 2004; Fahamu Ltd. for "The Making of an African NGO" by Issa G. Shivji, which is adapted from a special report titled "The Silences in the NGO Discourse: The Role and Future of NGOs in Africa" published by *Pambazuka News* in 2006; and Oxfam

GB (www.oxfam.org.uk) for "The Depoliticisation of Poverty" by Firoze Manji, which is adapted from *Development and Rights* (1998), a reader that is part of Oxfam GB's Development in Practice series (Oxfam GB does not necessarily endorse any texts or activities that accompany the materials presented in this anthology, nor has it approved the adapted text).

This anthology would also not have been possible without the inspiration provided by friends, colleagues and fellow writers, members of the Coalition of Concerned Kenyan Writers, in particular, who encouraged me to put together a collection of essays and articles that would present an alternative view of the development industry in Africa. I am especially grateful to the following people: Alain Dromsom, Shalini Gidoomal, Ali Zaidi and the Nordic Africa Institute, for commenting on the first draft of the manuscript; Muthoni Garland, Lucy Oriang, Dayo Forster, Muthoni Wanyeki, Kamal Shah, Neera Kapur-Dromsom and Aidan Hartley, for not thinking that I was crazy; Xavier Verhoest, for allowing me to using the image of his painting (which proudly hangs on my living room wall) on the cover; David Godwin, for providing valuable literary advice; Dean Shah, for guiding me through the publishing process; and most of all, to my husband Gray Phombeah, whose infinite patience astonishes me every single day.

Rasna Warah (Editor)

CONTENTS

INTRODUCTION:

PART ONE: DEVELOPMENT IN ACTION

PART TWO: THE DEVELOPMENT SET

PART THREE: THE POLITICS OF AID

INTRODUCTION

THE DEVELOPMENT MYTH

Rasna Warah

Development, as in Third World Development, is a debauched word, a whore of a word. Its users can't look you in the eye.

– **Leonard Frank,** *"The Development Game"*[1]

I first started having doubts about the relevance of the development industry during an interview that I was conducting with Mberita Katela, a woman living in Laini Saba, the densest and poorest section of Nairobi's Kibera slum, who earned an average daily income of 50 Kenya shillings (less than the proverbial dollar-a-day) selling *sukuma wiki* (kale) and cigarettes to her neighbours. It was March of 2002 and I had gone to Kibera to do what they call a "qualitative time-space analysis" of how slum dwellers spend their time and how much physical space they occupy while carrying out their daily chores. This activity was part of a larger and much broader global slum analysis being carried out by the United Nations Human Settlements Programme (UN-HABITAT), where I worked at the time.

As I sat on one of two small stools in Mberita's tiny wattle, daub and tin shack – which was only marginally bigger than my bathroom at home – I found myself asking her the most intimate details about her life, questions that I myself would not have entertained: what she ate for breakfast, how many people she shared her shack with and, most important of all, where she defecated. Through this exercise, I found out that she shared one stinking pit latrine with some 100 of her neighbours and that the latrine was located less than 10 metres from her shack, which she shared with her daughter and two grandchildren. Needless to say, the

3

stench of raw sewage permeated the air within and around her neighbourhood.

Mberita's story – or rather, the state of her living conditions – was published in a UN-HABITAT publication[2], and was subsequently picked up by the American author and urbanist Mike Davis, who used parts of the story in his provocative book *Planet of Slums*[3] to illustrate the dehumanising living conditions experienced by the world's urban poor. Meanwhile, Mberita has remained oblivious of the fact that her name now appears in a book, a magazine and in cyberspace (a Google search in February 2007 yielded 9 results). The publication of her story had little or no impact on her living conditions[4]; the most it did was create what development workers like to call "awareness" among some people and gained me a few Brownie points within the development fraternity. I had turned her into one of those people who, in the words of British columnist A.A. Gill, "slip through the cracks of good intentions" to become "slices of pie chart and exclamations".[5] I was sub-consciously doing what many people in the so-called development industry do: I was objectifying her, seeing her as part of a problem that needed to be solved so that she could be neatly compartmentalised into a "target group" category. This allowed me to perceive her as being "different" from me and bestowed on her an "otherness" that clearly placed her as my inferior, worthy of my sympathy.[6] Like most professionals working in the development industry, I had failed to see that my work and the structures within which I operated were self-serving.

Slum tourists

In recent years, Nairobi's slums have gained the attention of a host of celebrities, and Kibera has joined the rank of a "must-see" tourist site in Kenya, along with the Maasai Mara and Mount Kenya. U.S. Senator Barack Obama, former U.S. Secretary of State Madeleine Albright and Britain's Gordon Brown have all walked through the muck and human waste that pave Kibera's lanes. After Hollywood immortalised the slum in *The Constant Gardener*, interest in Kibera has grown so much that enterprising local travel agents have started including slum tours in their itineraries. One such travel agency, which even has a branch in Canada, offers what it calls the Kibera Slums Tour, along with honeymoon packages, luxury safaris and mountain hiking tours. The visit to Kibera is described as a "charity tour" where tourists are expected to contribute a minimum of $30 to orphanages, schools, HIV/Aids patients or individual slum households of their choice. Its website encourages visitors/philanthropists to take the tour with the following enticing (apparently unedited) lines:

> This tour is recommended for a business traveller(s), church missionary, a journalist(s), and a business executive who would like a quick feel of slum life in Kenya...Visit the Soweto Village homesteads, and then continue to the Curio (handcrafts) Workshop where you will witness how those living in Kibera slums are innovative in making ornaments out of animal bones. Continue with visits of the Nursery schools and pass by to the Water vender and the Shower shop as you meet other slum dwellers mingling with you as they carry on with their daily chores...Proceed to the other homesteads including those of the tour guides and security team members and witness their life styles in the slums. Pass by a popular pub within the slum for a drink, if you so wish, and pass over the bridge unto the Railway line. You may be lucky to witness the train pass on the railway line amidst the tin roofed houses with human beings and animals (goats, dogs, chickens crossing the railway line at the same time). Cross the railway line into the Centre housing the sick and share your moment with these deserving mothers and children of the slum.[7]

The sheer size of Kibera, which houses more than 600,000 people, and the depth of deprivation within it, elicit shock, horror and, at times, declarations of commitment. Visits to Kibera reached a crescendo during the 2007 World Social Forum held in Nairobi when anti-globalisation activists turned up at the slum to demonstrate their solidarity with the downtrodden. Kibera was also the first stop in United Nations Secretary-General Ban Ki-Moon's first official visit to Kenya in February 2007.

The slum residents, however, are not amused; "fact-finding" and goodwill missions to slums by celebrities and other "slum tourists" are seen by many as insulting. Car-washer David Kabala told *Reuters:* "They see us as puppets; they want to come and take pictures, have a little walk, tell their friends they've been to the worst slum in Africa. But nothing changes for us."[8] The *Daily Nation,* echoing the sentiments of Kabala, wondered whether this kind of "tourism" had any impact on the lives of slum residents. An editorial put forth the question: "What is this fascination with Kibera among people who do not know what real poverty means?"[9]

In other cities, such as Mumbai in India, a company has been running similar tours of Dharavi (dubbed "Asia's largest slum") since 2006. During the tour, travellers are taken to small-scale slum-based industries, such as recycling and tanning factories; an extra $8 will even buy them a ride through the city's notorious red-light district. Critics claim that such tours are merely voyeuristic attempts to allow tourists to gawk at Indian poverty and to take pictures.[10]

The death of development

A few years after my interview with Mberita, and after I had left the United Nations to pursue a writing career, I became increasingly obsessed with what is referred to as "post-development theory" – the notion that "development" as it is known today is a skewed concept that harms rather than benefits communities. If post-colonial literature recognises how "decolonised situations are marked by traces of the imperial pasts that they try to disavow"[11], post-development advocates try to render the development project irrelevant and detrimental to human progress. If development is "the management of a promise", as suggested by sociologist Jan Nederveen Pieterse, then post-development focuses on the underlying premises and motives of development. What sets it apart from other critical approaches is its rejection of development.[12]

Post-development advocates have not had a serious hearing in the last six decades. This is because since the birth of the United Nations in 1945, the notion of development has become a sacred cow within the international community, one that can not and must not be questioned. Not too long ago, when a dissident intellectual named Ivan Illich questioned the very idea of development (which he even had the audacity to refer to as "planned poverty"), he was quickly dismissed as a provocateur.[13] His ideas, however, were propagated by various critics of development, including the environmentalist and author Wolfgang Sachs, who claimed that "the idea of development stands like a ruin in the intellectual landscape" and that "delusion and disappointment, failures and crime have been the steady companions of development".[14] Sachs even went as far as saying, "It is not the failure of development that has to be feared, but its success."

These critics argued that development is more than a socio-economic endeavour; rather, it is "a perception that models reality, a myth that comforts societies and a fantasy that unleashes passion"[15].

In the past two decades, a variety of academics, economists and development practitioners, such as Susan George, Majid Rahnema, Arturo Escobar and Rajni Kothari, among others, have made concerted efforts to show the dangers inherent in current development paradigms and practices. Their arguments revolve around three basic premises:

1) That the development business and all those those who work for it are motivated by the need to impose new systems of domination on people of the Third World – in other words, that development is just another way that colonialism can be perpetuated without being labelled oppressive;

2) That development models, such as those imposed by the World Bank, the International Monetary Fund and other donor agencies, favour the rich at the expense of the poor and are, therefore, instrumental in perpetuating poverty in the so-called developing world; and

3) That the worldview, intentions and mindset of development practitioners are paternalistic, arrogant and totally ignorant of the reality of poor people's lives. The notion of "development" is also rejected because it is closely associated with "Westernisation".

The word development itself is fraught with self-negation. As the Mexican economist Gustavo Esteva (who calls himself "a deprofessionalised intellectual") observes, the word serves as a constant reminder to people in the so-called developing world of what they are not – i.e. developed. So almost all the people living in Africa, Asia and Latin America – regions that are not yet deemed to be "developed" – are assumed to be living in "an undesirable, undignified condition" that they can only escape by becoming "enslaved to other's experiences and dreams."[16]

Implicit in the word development is the idea that it is a state that can be achieved through technical interventions – more schools, more water points, more roads, more hospitals – that are only achievable through more aid. The UN system routinely labels countries as "least developed" or "developing" based on national data and statistics on income, literacy and longevity. This classification forms the basis of most UN and World Bank reports and is used by rich nations to determine which countries qualify for aid and debt relief. So modern-day Egypt, Iraq and India, places where civilisations thrived long before the birth of Christ, are now deemed "developing countries" by the vast pool of statisticians, demographers and economists employed by international development agencies. Countries and regions that were once pioneers of innovation, art, and science, whose people invented the wheel, operated complex irrigation systems and built architectural marvels such as the Taj Mahal, now happily accept this classification because it allows them to bargain more effectively for foreign aid.

Very few people in the development industry wonder why the biggest recipients of foreign aid, such as Ethiopia and Tanzania, remain among the most impoverished countries in the world. Failures of aid are largely attributed to corrupt governments, whose excesses can be curbed through what the World Bank terms as "conditionalities". No-one thinks of eliminating aid altogether. The small circle of academics and mavericks who question the effectiveness of aid and development assistance are by and large not taken seriously by the international development community. Their ideas may appear in some text books or speeches; they might even provoke discussion and debate within post-graduate courses and seminars, but they are seen as aberrations, lone voices in a world that is convinced that the ingredients of lifting the wretched of the earth out of poverty include higher economic growth, liberalised markets, good governance, better-funded NGOs and, most important of all, more aid.

As the veteran international development specialist Thomas W. Dichter has noted, organisations handling large amounts of money need structures through which the work and the money can be channelled; unfortunately, it is these same structures that limit and compromise development because, like many bureaucracies, the structures become more important than the work itself.[17] Moreover, unlike normal business ventures, the development industry is perhaps the only industry in the world where results – or the bottom line – do not determine whether or not it will survive. If results mattered, then many donor agencies and non-governmental organisations (NGOs) would have closed shop years ago when confronted with the fact that their work had neither reduced poverty in many countries, nor had it made people living in them less dependant on aid – which ultimately, should be the main objective of any organisation aiming to lift people out of poverty.

The trouble with Africa
Africa seems to elicit the lion's share of the world's foreign aid – and the world's sympathy – even though, in terms of absolute numbers, there are more poor people living in Asia, notwithstanding the recent economic successes of India and China. A World Bank pie chart on the distribution of people living on less than a dollar a day in

1998 showed that the whole of Asia was home to a whopping two-thirds of the world's poor; sub-Saharan Africa, on the other hand, hosted one quarter of the world's poorest people. [18] Yet there is no Bono or Bob Geldof trying to rescue Asia's teeming masses from death or disease. The "Make Poverty History Campaign", initiated in the U.K. in 2005, talked of doubling aid to Africa; no one bothered to request for increased aid to Asia, I assume, because Asia is considered to be a continent that knows how to lift itself up by its own bootstraps. For instance, in 2003, official development assistance received by sub-Saharan African countries amounted to $22.7 billion compared to $13.8 billion received by East and South Asia combined[19]. (This, however, does not include the aid that flows into Africa through international NGOs and private foundations, whose contributions are estimated to have surpassed those of bilateral donors in recent years.)

Although the proportion (not the number) of people living in back-breaking poverty is highest in Africa, the exclusive international focus on the continent may have to do with the fact that African problems are easier to "compartmentalise". Whether it is Aids, famine or conflict, Africa offers a canvas that can be painted into neat little boxes. "Because Africa seems unfinished and so different from the rest of the world, a landscape on which a person can sketch a new personality, it attracts mythomaniacs," observed Paul Theroux.[20]

Singer Madonna and Hollywood actress Angelina Jolie, who have made it their personal mission to adopt African babies, have added to the myths about Africa and fuelled the idea that all one needs to do to lift the continent out of poverty is to airlift its babies to Europe or America. This attitude was epitomised recently by the six members of the French charity Zoe's Ark, who were arrested and convicted by Chadian authorities in December 2007 for attempting to "kidnap" 103 Chadian children and fly them out to France. The charity workers insisted throughout their trial that their main mission was to place the children – who they believed were orphans from strife-torn Darfur – in foster care with French families. However, independent investigations by the United Nations and other agencies revealed that most of the children were neither orphans nor were they from Darfur. The UN children's agency, Unicef, even accused the aid workers of breaching international law. Questions were raised about whether the charity was, in fact, a child trafficking agency.[21]

Whether or not the charity workers were innocent is almost beside the point: the point is, who gave these people the authority to dip into an African country and pick up children at will? Their approach to Africa's problems was as simplistic as that of the 17-year American student who, when asked why she wanted to go to Africa, is reported to have said, "There are a lot of problems (in Africa), but you can group them together. I can organise Africa in my head, in terms of poverty, droughts, even governments."[22]

Apparently, organising Asia in one's head is not as easy, what with its ancient cultures and its arrogant and stubborn governments, which are becoming increasingly sceptical about foreigners meddling in their affairs. For instance, when the Indian Ocean tsunami devastated several parts of Indonesia, Sri Lanka, Thailand and India in December 2004, the Indian government refused any kind of foreign humanitarian assistance, even though the country's eastern coast was among the worst affected regions. On the contrary, India offered aid to other affected countries, a move that was seen by many as a gesture indicating that it viewed itself as a regional superpower that did not need handouts from foreigners.

African governments have no hang-ups about begging for foreign aid; in fact, many measure their success by their ability to attract foreign funds. Some sub-Saharan African countries even base the bulk of their national budgets on remittances by foreign donors, not on domestic revenues. It is only in recent years that countries such as Kenya have weaned themselves away from donor-funded budgeting, an achievement that Kenya's Finance Minister loves to boast about on the annual Budget Day.[23] The national budgets of neighbouring Uganda and

Tanzania, however, are still very much tied to how much donors contribute to them.

The resultant loss of sovereignty is a huge price to pay considering that official development assistance (ODA) – money that governments of advanced economies designate for foreign aid programmes – comprises less than 1 per cent of rich countries' Gross National Product (GNP). Taxpayers in the United States, Sweden, the United Kingdom or Japan hardly feel the pinch, but the recipients of aid – African governments and the African people – not only feel the pinch, they ache from it for several years after it has been inflicted. The discomfort is hardly worth it because the amount of aid that goes to Africa is a drop in the ocean compared to what rich countries have been spending on defence in recent years. By May of 2007, for instance, it was estimated that the U.S. Congress had approved a total of $510 billion since the U.S. government began its global war on terror in 2001 (roughly $85 billion a year), most of it to fund the wars in Iraq and Afghanistan.[24] This is almost the total amount of aid that Africa has received from donor countries in the last 40 years. What is worse is that this kind of defence spending does little to boost development in the countries where it is spent. For example, Pakistan, one of the bigger beneficiaries of the U.S. war on terror, has been receiving up to $150 million a month in American aid, ostensibly to fight Al Qaeda, yet 2 out of every 3 women in Pakistan remain illiterate.[25]

Aid-dependency also ensures that rich countries retain some control over their former colonies. When the aid is given in the form of a loan (which normally comes with stringent and often punitive conditionalities attached), the control is easier to exercise. As Susan George, author of *A Fate Worse Than Debt* put it:

Debt is not a financial problem. It is a political problem. If you cancelled all the debt of the poorest countries tomorrow, the international financial system would not even notice. However, debt is extraordinarily useful for the North; it is much better than colonialism as you don't need an army etc.

to keep people in line, and you don't need the people. But you get tremendous political advantage because you have continuous low prices for raw materials, everyone is forced to export at the same time, and you have political control over the government.[26]

Dependency on aid also allows development workers and other do-gooders to continue justifying to themselves why their work is so important. Visits to Kibera and other sites of degrading poverty offer them an opportunity to ease their conscience and to gloss over the fact that foreign debt, imposed economic reforms, unfair trade policies, corrupt governments, not to mention centuries of slavery and colonialism, are among the main causes of poverty in Africa – not the lack of sufficient foreign aid.

China's recent engagement with Africa, if not monitored closely, could also end up perpetuating poverty on the continent. The difference between the Chinese and the Western approach to development in Africa, however, is that the Chinese do not view Africa's development as charity, but as a business opportunity. The Chinese do not couch their aid with words such as "development" or "good governance"; they are more likely than their Western counterparts to admit that investing in African infrastructure and other projects is in their national political and economic interest, as the continent provides a substantial proportion of the raw materials needed to maintain China's booming economy. Nor do they suffer from pangs of guilt every time they are confronted with African poverty, maybe because they have been there – they know what poverty means. As a young American woman who has spent many months in China explained to me: "When *mzungus* (white people) see a barefoot African child on a dirt road in his village, they call the number on the bottom of the screen and give a dollar – a sort of instant absolution at a very bargain price. A Chinese sees that same image and sees a market of one billion consumers who need one billion pairs of shoes."[27]

Corrupt elite and failing institutions

UN reports routinely report that many African countries are poorer now than they were in 1980, at the end of what was dubbed "the second UN Development Decade", despite being among the biggest recipients of official development assistance in the last 40 years.[28] Despite impressive economic growth rates in recent years, growth in most African countries has failed to trickle down to the poorest groups. In Nairobi, for instance – the city that hosts the UN agency charged with improving the lot of slum dwellers worldwide – slums have become worse places to live than they were three decades ago. In 1971, eight years after Kenya achieved independence, there were 50 informal settlements, or slums, in the city housing less than 200,000 people; today there are almost 200 slums in the city where an estimated 1.8 million people – more than half the city's population – live.[29] More than 60 per cent of sub-Saharan Africa's urban population lives in slums such as Kibera, where people like Mberita eke out an existence with no running water, no electricity, and no breathing space.[30]

Although the growth of slums in African cities is the result of a variety of factors, including rapid urbanisation and the after-effects of the World Bank-IMF-led structural adjustment programmes of the late 1980s and 1990s, which reduced or eliminated subsidies on basic services in urban areas, their growth is also symptomatic of a deeper reality: without slums, many cities in Africa would not function. African cities rely on the relatively cheap labour provided by slum dwellers to man their factories, to construct buildings, to clean their streets and to generally make the economy grow. Slum dwellers, in turn, need the employment generated by cities to survive, and they need affordable housing (provided by slums) to be able to compete in a job market where labour is cheap and where rents for better housing are unaffordable. (Recent research shows that the average monthly rent paid for a one-bedroom flat in Umoja, a low-income neighbourhood in Nairobi, is approximately 7000 Kenya shillings, or $100, slightly more than the average monthly income of a Kibera resident.[31]) Slums are, therefore, sites of immense opportunity and enterprise, where dreams of escaping poverty are first nurtured – even if, in their present condition, they are also sites of life-threatening diseases and environmental degradation brought on by lack of basic services such as water and sanitation.

This does not mean, however, that the presence of huge slums in African cities must be tolerated – condemning such large numbers of people to dehumanising living conditions for long periods of time is not just unethical but economically unviable. People who are vulnerable to early death and disease and who live in deplorable living conditions do not make good workers i.e. their contribution to the economy is hampered by their poor health and by the time and energy burden that most carry from not having easy access to water, sanitation, affordable transport and other services. Slums epitomise the failure of governance institutions; they will only stop growing when there is sustained political will to adopt an integrated, multi-sectoral approach, using government resources, to upgrade them and provide them with basic services and infrastructure at subsidised rates. Moreover, sustained economic growth will only have an impact on the poorest groups when it is linked to eliminating corruption, distributing resources more equitably and making housing more affordable for the poorest groups – a much more ambitious and risky endeavour that many African governments are not yet willing to undertake.

More importantly, African countries need to develop institutions and human resources to sustain economic growth and to improve the living standards of the majority. But, as many of the contributors to this anthology have pointed out, the development of efficient and effective institutions and human resources is hampered by none other than the largely corrupt African political elite – one of the biggest causes of underdevelopment in the region.

Dichter believes that development in Africa has failed because it has been targeting the wrong things in the wrong way:

Development professionals continue to hedge the question of whether development assistance is about doing things. Increasingly we know that the keys to development are neither tangible nor involve much 'doing'. They are about institutions, attitudes, laws and human resources. And yet we continue to 'do' development as if it were largely about doing things and doing those things, moreover, for others. If development professionals were successful in fostering institutions, attitudes, and laws and in enhancing human resources, we – as professional developers – would not have to do things like build schools or roads. The institutions of a functioning society would see to it that they got built.[32]

The 3 Ms

This anthology brings together a range of "development cynics" who have learned first-hand or through observation about the failures of the development business as it is practised today. The various contributors to this book not only question whether current development practice is good for Africa and the rest of the so-called developing world, but also critique the mindset, intentions and worldviews of the organisations that have made Africa their business, including bilateral and multilateral donor agencies, non-governmental organisations (NGOs), humanitarian agencies and most importantly, African governments, which have become the leadings chanters of the development mantra, but who do everything in their power to keep the continent poor.

The authors who have contributed to this book are an eclectic mix; here, among others, you will find a leftist scholar who unveils what he calls "the silences in the NGO discourse", a banker who urges African governments to "grow up" and stop begging for more donor aid, a BBC correspondent who critiques the lifestyles of development workers in Africa and an investigative journalist who uncovers the post-colonial machinations of Kenya's political elite against the Maasai community. All the contributors to this anthology approach the notion of development through their own worldviews and experiences; many are convinced that it is time to declare the death of development as an idea, as an ideology, and as an industry.

The book is not so ambitious as to offer alternatives to development, "ways forward" or prescriptions. Any such attempt would necessarily be based on the idea that human progress can be socially engineered through "best practice" models and carefully controlled interventions by outsiders or that development can be measured through narrow indicators such as Gross Domestic Product (GDP), literacy and longevity. The intention of this book is to take a focused peep into the development industry as it is practised in Africa and to expose the reader to a much-needed African perspective on the development industry and why it has failed so miserably in lifting the continent's people out of poverty.

This anthology would not have been possible without my fellow writers, journalists, development workers and activists who allowed me to use their brilliant essays that offer a glimpse of a vision gone terrible wrong; hopefully, these essays will form the basis of much-needed dialogue and debate on the myth and reality of the development industry.

The title of this book comes from a conversation I had with a humanitarian aid worker in Kabul in the winter of 2002, a few months after a US-led coalition had ousted the Taliban "government" from the city. It was a strange time to be in Afghanistan. I was representing one of at least 20 UN organisations that had descended on the war-torn country, armed with proposals and strategies to assist a near-medieval society to join the development bandwagon. Humanitarian aid workers, international NGOs and foreign correspondents who had never set foot in the country during its 20 years of conflict were in Kabul to document the face of poverty and oppression. The UN, the kingpin of all humanitarian efforts in the country, coordinated all their movements.

Part of the UN strategy to safeguard the lives of all the do-gooders in the country was to house them all under one roof. Because there was no functioning hotel in the city, we were forced to live in the UN guesthouse, a dormitory-style building in the centre of the city, which also happened to be the only place where one could buy an alcoholic drink. Patrons at the bar downstairs comprised the Who's Who of the development set. Heads of UN agencies mingled with regional directors of bilateral and multilateral donor agencies. Television reporters exchanged notes with humanitarian aid workers. Almost all of them were concerned with mainly one thing – how to get Afghan women to take off those damn *burqas*.

One crisp, chilly night, when I went downstairs for my daily shot of whisky – the only spirit available in the country – I bumped into a young Canadian who appeared as bewildered as I was. I was the only non-white person in the bar, and to make it worse, I was dressed in a *salwaar kameez* (loose top and pants commonly worn by men and women in northern India, Pakistan and Afghanistan) that I had purchased in Islamabad a few days before, partly because the airline had lost my luggage, and also because I felt I needed to respect the local culture by dressing modestly. The international development set thought I was a local, so they ignored me. The only person who struck up a conversation with me was this disillusioned development worker (whose name I forget) from Canada who it appeared was beginning to question his chosen profession.

In a room full of animated journalists, aid workers and UN honchos who were either boasting loudly about their life-threatening experiences in Afghanistan or discussing their multimillion dollar plans to improve women's health, women's reproductive rights, women's access to education, women's political participation and whatever else they thought the oppressed *burqa*-clad women of Afghanistan needed, the quiet Canadian offered a welcome relief from all the chatter. After introducing himself, he casually asked me, "So which category do you place yourself under? Missionary, mercenary or misfit?" I never quite answered his question but it did lead to me to undertake a journey that culminates in this book, which I dedicate to that Canadian whose name I may never know.

Notes

1 Frank, Leonard (1997), "The Development Game", *The Post-Development Reader*, London and New York: Zed Books Ltd.

2 Warah, Rasna (2002), "Nairobi's Slums: Where Life for Women is Nasty, Brutish and Short", *Habitat Debate*, Vol. 8 No. 4, December.

3 Davis, Mike (2006), *Planet of Slums*, London and New York: Verso.

4 Mberita Katela's living conditions may not have improved, but she has been involving herself in various community activities since I last spoke to her. A newspaper report in March 2008 named her as the chairperson of an environmental initiative in Kibera called Ushirika was Usafi Laini Saba.

5 Gill, A.A. (2005), "Eye Witness" *Sunday Times* magazine, 3 July.

6 Interview with Mberita Katela conducted by the author in March 2002.

7 www.victoriasafaris.com/kenyatours/kiberaslumtours.htm, accessed on 4 November 2007.

8 Cawthorne, Andrew (2007), "Slum Tourism Stirs a Storm in Kenya", *Reuters*, 13 February.

9 *Daily Nation*, "Kibera is no tourist site" 2 February 2007

10 Shahid, Aliyah (2008), "Slum tourism or reality tours, opinion is split", HT Media Ltd., 12 March.

11 Gikandi, Simon (1996), *Maps of Englishness: Writing Identity in the Culture of Colonialism*. New York: Columbia University Press.

12 Picterse, Nederveen Jan (2001) *Development Theory: Deconstructions/Reconstructions*, London, Thousand Oaks, CA, New Delhi: SAGE Publications Ltd.

13 Illich, Ivan (1997). In *The Post-Development Reader* (Eds. Rahnema, M. and Bawntree, V.), London and New Jersey: Zed Books.

14 Sachs, Wolfgang (Ed.) (1992) "Introduction", *The Development Dictionary*, London and New York: Zed Books.

15 Ibid.

16 Esteva, Gustavo (1992) In: "Development", *The Development Dictionary*, London and New York: Zed Books.

17 Dichter, Thomas W. (2003), *Despite Good Intentions: Why Development Assistance to the Third World Has Failed*, Amherst and Boston: University of Massachusetts Press.

18 World Bank (2000), *World Development Report 2000/2001: Attacking Poverty*, Washington DC: Oxford University Press, figure 1

19 UNDP (2005) *Human Development Report 2005*, table 19.

20 Quoted in Williams, Alex (2006), "Into Africa", *New York Times*, 13 August.

[21] Reuters (2007), "Chad spells out terms for handing over aid workers", 27 December.

[22] Quoted in Williams, Alex (2006).

[23] Kenya's donor-independence suffered a severe setback in early 2008, when the country was on the brink of a civil war after a flawed election. Donors are now an integral part of the country's rebuilding efforts.

[24] Congressional Research Service, quoted in *TIME* 14 May 2007.

[25] Baker, Aryn (2007), "Bhutto Unshackled", *TIME,* November 26.

[26] George, Susan (1998), *A Fate Worse Than Debt*: Grove Press.

[27] Jen Brea, the author of this quote, says she decided to go to China to "witness the birth of an empire" because she herself was born in an empire that had gone terribly wrong. E-mail correspondence, various dates between August 2007 and February 2008.

[28] UNDP (2005) *Human Development Report 2005: International Cooperation at a Crossroads*, New York.

[29] Government of Kenya-United Nations Centre for Human Settlements (2001), "Nairobi Situation Analysis: Collaborative Nairobi: Slum Upgrading Initiative".

[30] UN-HABITAT (2006), *State of the World's Cities Report 2006/7*, London and Sterling, VA: Earthscan.

[31] Huchzermeyer, Marie (2006), "Slum upgrading initiatives in Kenya within the basic services and wider housing market: A housing rights concern", Discussion paper No. 1/2006, COHRE Africa Programme, Geneva.

Part 1:
DEVELOPMENT IN ACTION

1

JOURNEY TO NOWHERE

Victoria Schlesinger

On an oppressively hot morning in January 2006, I set out in a rented car from Kisumu, an aging port city on the shores of Lake Victoria, to visit Sauri, a remote outcropping of farming villages in the northwestern corner of Kenya's Nyanza province. I was travelling to Sauri with a simple goal: to witness the beginning of the end of global poverty.

The narrow two-lane highway to Sauri cuts a winding path through the region's abundant maize and sugarcane fields, from which I could just barely discern the outline of mud-and-thatch homesteads, connected by a jagged patchwork of red-dirt roads and footpaths. Old women balancing oversize buckets of water on their heads and men in dirty sports jackets riding bicycles saddled with 200-pound bags of maize gave way as my car sped by. Shirtless youths burdened with unwieldy loads of brush piled high atop their heads stared wordlessly as I passed, and when young children caught sight of me they yelled, sometimes in fear, sometimes in glee, *"Mzungu, mzungu!"* ("White person!").

Sauri is actually a tightly-knit constellation of eleven small hamlets with a total population of about 5,000. Most Saurians observe a mixture of Christianity and traditional Luo religion, which means they both revere the Bible and practise polygamy. Famous for their lyrical music and dance, the Luo are among the poorest ethnic groups in Kenya and have historically been discriminated against by the Kikuyus, the country's largest and most politically powerful tribe. The Luo are the largest tribal group in Nyanza province, an area where 65 per cent of the population lives in severe poverty, nearly a quarter of the children under the age of five suffer from malnutrition, and 20 per cent are orphans. This leaves Nyanza's Luo among the poorest in an already poor country: at least 50 per cent of Kenya's 35 million people live below the poverty line; one out of ten children dies before the age of five, most of them from disease; more than 2 million people are infected with HIV; 2 million have died from complications related to HIV/Aids.

Grim statistics such as these led economist Jeffrey Sachs – special advisor to former United Nations Secretary-General Kofi Annan and director of Columbia University's Earth Institute – to choose Sauri as the location for the first research village of the Millennium Villages Project (MVP), an endeavour whose stated goal is to halve the number of people living on less than a dollar a day in sub-Saharan Africa by 2015. Sachs, named one of the hundred "most influential" people in the world by *Time* magazine in 2005 and best known professionally for his "shock therapy" approach to fixing the post-Communist economies of Russia and Poland, is also the author of the much-lauded 2005 bestseller *The End of Poverty* (foreword by Bono). In the book, Sachs claims that the world's intractable systemic poverty could be resolved, efficiently and quickly, via a package of inexpensive, scientifically-based solutions, all for as little as $110 per person annually. Sachs founded the first Millennium Village in Sauri in 2004, and it has since expanded into 11 other research villages in ten African countries, plus an additional 66 villages that receive similar aid but are only monitored. Along with his colleagues at the Earth Institute, Sachs envisions the villages spreading across the entire African continent, creating "a scalable model for fighting poverty that can be expanded from the village to district level and eventually to additional countries".

First impressions
It took about an hour, much of it spent driving on a rutted dirt road, to reach my first destination, Sauri's new medical clinic. Constructed with MVP money, the freshly painted five-room building stood adjacent to the row of

squat, single-room structures that make up the Sauri community centre. The centre was home to a meeting room used by the villagers and also had plans for a computer lab and a library. I peered inside one of the boxy, white-washed rooms, empty but for a few pieces of furniture and a small purple desk, above which was a sign that read: PROPOSED COMPUTER TABLE 1.

Outside the clinic, several dozen people sat on light blue benches in the shade of a tin awning, waiting to be seen. Decorative green-and-red leaved plants sat on either side of the door marked LABORATORY in black, stencilled letters. Inside, I met a smiling young man who introduced himself as Jared Oule, a nurse from Kenya's Ministry of Health on loan to the MVP. Inviting us into his tiny lab, which was stocked with a generator-powered refrigerator and microscopes for analysing blood samples, Oule happily rattled off a list of MVP community-development projects underway: the distribution of seeds and fertilizer to local farmers; the expansion of an already existing school free-lunch programme; a programme to oversee the use of the community's newly acquired two-door Nissan pickup; the construction of cisterns to protect surrounding spring water from contamination; the creation of a business plan for a local café; even a proposal for providing Internet access to the villagers, "once the government extends the power grid here".

The following morning, I made my way to a nearby Anglican church for a meeting with the Sauri Executive Committee, a liaison group that coordinates activities among the MVP's numerous committees. The first person I met was the chairperson, Monica Okech. A stout, grandmotherly woman in her fifties, Okech constituted a fine example of what could be called an "upper middle class" Saurian; this meant she had enough money to construct a concrete-walled and tin-roofed house, and she was able to regularly hire workers to farm her land.

Okech began to tell me the history of Sauri's involvement with international aid groups, which, to my surprise, was a long one; Sauri has received financial assistance from international organisations for more than 15 years. The

World Agroforestry Centre and the Kenya Agricultural Research Institute have conducted projects here since 1991; Africa Now, a U.K.-based charity, came to Sauri in the late nineties to build spring-protection cisterns; a women's credit cooperative started by CARE Kenya in 1999 was still underway; and the free-lunch programme, initiated by the local school principal, had been feeding students since 2000. This struck me as somewhat odd. Given the wealth of ongoing development work, Sauri appeared to be a less than ideal choice as the site of a test case for poverty eradication aimed at the "poorest of the poor". If one were truly attempting to establish a representative baseline of data for the MVP model, would it not be more logical to choose an untouched locale?

The MVP has taken a decidedly different approach, relying instead on pilot sites with what it considers the highest likelihood of success rather those that exemplify the depth of the problem. Half of the research villages have been situated in areas with an established history of interaction with foreign development groups. The idea is that the likelihood of rapid success is greater in places such as these because inexperience with and cultural barriers against development work have already been overcome.

My conversation with Okech was cut short by the arrival of two men. Patrick Mutuo, a portly, boyish-faced Kenyan whom I recognised from the MVP website as the local project manager, was the first, followed by MVP project director and renowned agronomist Pedro Sanchez. Okech warmly greeted Sanchez, whom she has known since the mid-1990s, when he first came to Sauri as the director-general of the World Agroforestry Centre. Sanchez was in Sauri to prepare for the visit of a group of financial donors who would be accompanied by Jeffrey Sachs. He indicated to Okech that he wanted to take a tour of the crop fields. Okech invited me to accompany them.

It was close to noon by the time we reached the fields, and the sky above Sauri was filled with billowy white clouds that offered little promise of rain. Kenya had suffered a harsh drought during the shorter of its two rainy seasons. Crops had failed both in Sauri and nationwide. Sanchez, his sun hat pulled down snugly and his mouth a grim straight line, surveyed the small valley of farms behind the church. The maize plots were little more than a desiccated mess of stalks and leaves dried to the consistency of brown shipping paper. Okech and the other Kenyans with us looked sombre and uncomfortable. Okech stood at Sanchez's side, her features flat and serious as she worried a sprig of guava leaves in her strong farmer's hands and explained, with another extension officer translating, the severity of the situation in Sauri: the harvest would be an utter failure.

"But no one is Sauri will go hungry," Sanchez pronounced rather loudly. He was referring to the harvest of July 2005, a bumper crop that Sachs, during a "thinkMTV" documentary featuring Angelina Jolie, had called "an incredible triumph". Okech, her unease visibly increasing, replied that some in the community had been forced to sell their maize to pay for other needs, like building supplies, funerals, rent and school fees. They had no household surplus and soon would be without food.

"There is a surplus," Sanchez said firmly. "The committee should distribute the surplus." Okech explained that some members of the committee in charge of the reserve didn't want to distribute it. They believed that those now in need were at fault – because they were either lazy, didn't want to follow correct planting procedures, or had acted against MVP recommendations, which urged participating villagers to use their maize for food or sell it to the MVP cereal bank. This faction of the committee opposed bailing out farmers they considered unwilling to follow the MVP plan. Okech feared that fighting might erupt among villagers when the decision was made as to who would be helped.

"The community should help these people," Sanchez said softly. "No one should be hungry in Sauri."

We continued on to the other fields, Okech fiddling with the broken watch she wore on her wrist as jewellery while Sanchez maintained a pensive silence. We had reached a parched soybean field when Sanchez, clearly shaken by the sight of the failed crops, announced that he'd "seen enough".

"It's better in other locations," Mutuo suggested.

"We'll go to those places for the visitors," Sanchez answered. "We need to impress these people."

Our last stop was outside a local school, where we stood staring at an unplanted field. Okech suggested that Sanchez and the MVP offer micro-credit to defray some of the farm overhead, by which she meant basic things like paying workers, repairing tools, or, for those with small plots, renting land. Many villagers, she said, had sold the maize from last year's bumper crop to pay for these expenses. To this, Sanchez, winner of the 2002 World Food Prize and recipient of a MacArthur Foundation "genius" grant that includes a $500,000 "no strings attached" award, responded by saying, "I don't understand why they need money to prepare their land." He paused and chuckled self-consciously. "Maybe that's a stupid question."

The beginning of the end of poverty?

On September 18, 2000, the United Nations issued the Millennium Development Declaration, a laudably altruistic set of principles that included eradicating extreme hunger and poverty, the promotion of gender equality, the achievement of universal primary education, and the pursuit of the fight against Aids and malaria. If successful, the declaration's goals were to be reached by 2015 and would represent an unprecedented lessening of worldwide misery.

The wealthy nations of the world hastened to get involved. In 2002, the European Union and the United States made a pledge (albeit a non-binding one) to donate 0.7 per cent of their respective GNPs toward aid for developing countries. The following year, the United States created the Millennium Challenge Corporation, which has dispersed more than $1.5 billion in grants to Africa, and pledged another $15 billion toward HIV/Aids relief. In 2005, the European Union set a target of 66 billion euros annually to developing nations by 2010, with Britain alone providing more than 1 billion pounds to sub-

Saharan Africa in 2006. The year before, the G8 nations cancelled roughly $40 billion in debt for the world's poorest countries, most of which are in Africa. Large non-profit organisations took action as well. The Global Fund to Fight Aids, Tuberculosis and Malaria has contributed $3.2 billion to date; the Bill and Melinda Gates Foundation donated $287 million for HIV/Aids research and $750 million for vaccines and immunization of impoverished children; in 2006, Warren Buffet gave another $30 billion to the Gates Foundation.

Although this outpouring of financial largesse is admirable, the history of Western generosity and grand solutions in Africa does not bode well for its future success. Economist William Easterly, an outspoken critic of U.S. foreign aid policy and author of the recent book *The White Man's Burden*, estimates that the developed nations have donated $568 billion in aid to Africa since the 1960s. Yet the poverty has only worsened. The population of sub-Saharan Africans living on less than a dollar a day rose from 41 to 46 per cent between 1981 and 2001 – which means that there are an additional 150 million people living in dire circumstances. Presently, the life expectancy of sub-Saharan Africa's 750 million people stands at just 46 years.

Economists, politicians and academics of every stripe have offered explanations for the intransigence of African poverty, perhaps none more vociferously than Sachs, who took centre stage in the debate when Kofi Annan appointed him to head the UN Millennium Project. Sachs's first task was to oversee the preparation of an "action plan" on how best to achieve the Millennium Development Goals (commonly known as MDGs), a process that brought him into close contact with Pedro Sanchez, who along with Sanchez's wife, Cheryl Palm (also an accomplished agronomist), was responsible for the report on hunger. From the plan's findings came the first rough outline of what, in 2004, would become the Millennium Villages Project.

Sachs rarely shies away from highlighting the revolutionary aspects of the MVP and its efforts in Sauri. "This is a village that's going to make history," he said in the MTV documentary. "It's a village that's going to end extreme poverty." The MVP would attempt to simultaneously augment agricultural yields, increase access to clean water and sanitation, and improve basic health care, schools and the infrastructure. This approach, Sachs reasoned, would be the most reliable means of creating an economic cushion that would buffer the poor against ever-present problems such as drought and illness. Millennium Promise calls Sauri and its peer villages "a ground-breaking concept" in village-level anti-poverty development, which will succeed because of its commitment to "Doing all of it, all at once."

Despite the sweeping rhetoric, the MVP is hardly the first attempt at spurring radical rural economic growth through an all-at-once approach. Efforts to jump-start an agricultural revolution through a "holistic package" of improvements took place in many locations, under a wide variety of circumstances, during the 1970s and 1980s, under the rubric of Integrated Rural Development, or IRD. Proponents of this method believed that only a Green Revolution, like that of India and Mexico, would be forceful enough to pull the increasingly disenfranchised rural poor into the mainstream productive sectors of developing economies. To achieve this end required not only investment in agriculture – better seeds, fertilizer, and access to markets – but also improvements in health and education services. Attempts to implement the IRD model were made throughout the developing world, with funding from institutions such as USAID, the World Bank and UNDP, as well as large private donors, including the Ford and Rockefeller foundations. It was also backed by nations such as Britain, Sweden, Norway and the Netherlands.

Oddly enough, Sanchez, who I met again at the Earth Institute in New York after I visited Sauri, didn't have much to say about IRD, because of what he called "very little analysis" of the old projects. "We just don't have the data," he said.

However, a search for the term "integrated rural development" in the library database at Columbia University – where Sanchez works – brought forth 165 hits on the topic; the USAID database delivered another 704; the World Bank's website, 125. With little effort, I was able to order in-depth project reports and evaluations that charted the spotty history of IRD and rural poverty: in Swaziland, an agricultural rural-development programme conducted throughout the 1970s foundered in the wake of government incompetence and opposition; Save the Children's five-year Tunisian village IRD project concluded in 1983; an IRD project in Sudan funded by USAID dissolved amid political instability. By the mid-1980s, the concept of IRD had fallen into disrepute.

Kenya's experiment with IRD dates to the early 1970s, with the implementation of the Special Rural Development Programme (SRDP), which attempted to make simultaneous improvements to the health, education, agriculture, and infrastructure sectors. Assessment of the SRDP found that few, if any, new anti-poverty ideas emerged from these experimental projects; they were burdened with large recurring costs and were not self-sustaining. In Kenya, as elsewhere, researchers noted that while specific factors, such as insufficient technology, experts and money, had handicapped IRD, overwhelmingly the primary cause of failure was lack of cooperation between donors and recipient governments. The 1976 book *Aid and Inequality in Kenya* noted that government officials viewed the SRDP as an "expatriate show", suitable only as a "device for getting aid donors to commit untied funds". By the late 1970s, the Kenyan government had entirely abandoned the SRDP, which had been implemented nationwide, acknowledging that it had made little progress toward improving the lot of the country's rural poor.

VIPs in SUVs

Four days later, as the roads began to fill with women and men carrying their heavy morning loads, the MVP impresarios and their donors arrived in Sauri to observe the progress. The group numbered roughly 25 VIPs, plus their drivers, translators, and security guards, transported in a convoy of safari vehicles and four-wheel-drive SUVs. Among them were New York Yankees co-owner Ray

Chambers, co-founder with Sachs of the Millennium Promise nonprofit; Ben Goldhirsh, the 26-year-old millionaire founder of *Good*, a magazine whose original mission statement boasted that the "world of good" is "not just for do-gooders any more"; a representative from the Case Foundation in Washington D.C., which had already donated considerable funds to the project; and Rieko Suzuki Kitaoka, wife of a senior Japanese diplomat to the United Nations, who arrived dressed in pristine white jeans and a black straw sun hat, and who said she was there as "a friend of Jeff and Sonia's". In the back seat of a white SUV sat Sachs, his wife, Dr. Sonia Ehrlich Sachs, and their youngest daughter.

By midmorning, the convoy had reached Yala township near Sauri and made its way to the communal storage property, parking before a row of giant corrugated-metal and concrete warehouses used to hold grain. Climbing from their vehicles, the VIPs resembled nothing so much as a flash flood of khaki sweeping across the road, a rogue wave of sunglasses and sunhats imperilling the small band of Sauri villagers in their Sunday finest – the executive committee – waiting to greet them.

Sachs greeted Okech, who, swathed in a matching aquamarine tie-dyed dress, scarf and head wrap, stepped forward and warmly embraced him, happily repeating "Hello" and "How are you?" in broken English. When Patrick Mutuo presented Okech to the VIPs, she responded by spreading her arms wide and saying in Luo, "Welcome, to my teachers and God." Okech then introduced each executive committee member and was halfway through thanking them for making the long trip to her village when I noticed a few of the VIPs jerk uncomfortably like fish leaping out of water. Looking down, I saw swarm of large black ants scurrying hurly-burly through the red dust beneath us, crawling around and over VIP leather loafers and strappy black sandals. It seemed we were standing on their mound, crushing their colony and trails. Okech, apparently undaunted by the bugs, pressed on with her speech, while the donors shifted uncomfortably and swatted at their ankles.

Safely inside the immense, cobweb-stippled storage house, the VIPs admired the bulging white plastic maize sacks covering the floor. I wondered why some sacks were stacked flat in piles of three while others were propped up on end. A committee member dressed in a suit and tie explained that the upright sacks, 10 per cent of the total harvest, would be donated to the school free-lunch programme. The 281 sacks lying flat contained the cereal-bank community reserve that Okech and Sanchez had discussed earlier. The MVP had purchased the maize from Sauri farmers for roughly $16 per sack, then sold it on their behalf at a $4 profit when the maize was scarce on the local market.

One of the committee members began to talk to the VIPs about the maize. In 2005, he said, the MVP had supplied Sauri's farmers with 8 tonnes of high-quality hybrid maize seeds and 120 tonnes of chemical fertilizer. Five months later, Sauri harvested the largest maize crop in history – 956 tonnes. Average crop yields increased 150 per cent, from 2 to 5 tonnes per hectare, and Sauri's farmers planted an additional 100 hectares. Sachs had mentioned the harvest during an address he made at the United Nations in September 2005, calling it "a tremendous achievement" and ample evidence that the only obstacle to meeting the Millennium Declaration's goals was political will and money.

Perhaps. But after my visit to Sauri, I spoke to Dickson Khainga, an economist at the Kenya Institute for Public Policy Research and Analysis, a think tank that advises Kenya's national government. Khainga described the MVP approach as "just proving what we know" – namely, that with an influx of fertilizer and money, farmers working nutrient-depleted soil can expect significant yield increases. "If we invest well in the farm," he said, "(we) will raise more. I think the main underlying issue is why it is that we don't do what we know."

At the UN, Sachs failed to mention that the chemical fertilizers that produced this abundance would be greatly de-emphasised in the future. After that, the MVP planned for Sauri's farmers to gradually replace the chemicals with a natural fertilizer shrub called a fallow. Although long advocated by development experts as a cost-efficient way to fertilize soil, fallows, unlike chemical fertilizers, require a specific combination of education, technical support and patience, and there is no guarantee that farmers will continue to use them. Sanchez had in fact introduced fallows to Sauri in 1996 as part of a pilot programme for the World Agroforestry Centre. By 2004, he noted, only a dozen farmers continued to plant them.

The bumper harvest provided villagers with a supply of maize to sell, store or eat. But, as Okech had already informed Sanchez, those with small plots were unable to grow enough to pay their expenses and move beyond the threat of hunger. This fact should have come as no surprise to Sanchez. According to MVP data, the much-improved yields would provide the average Sauri farm with roughly 63 bags of maize annually. Selling these bags to the MVP cereal bank, a family would earn about $1,260, enough to meet the dollar-a-day threshold for only half a year.

Next we stopped at the government-owned Yala sub-district hospital. Unlike the MVP clinic, this was a single-storey cement building with filthy walls, peeling paint, and a slew of outdoor benches crowded with dull-eyed patients. The hospital, which provides care for as many as 96,000 people, had no surgical theatre, no running water, and just 16 beds. Inside, the few metal cots were arranged in a row as in an army medical ward. Two, three, and four sick people lay listlessly next to one another, crowded onto one green vinyl mattress. Women hovered around their supine children, offering them water from grimy plastic jugs, and skeletal young men suffering from HIV/Aids sat on the concrete floor waiting to be seen by a doctor.

The host for the hospital tour was Steven Biko, a young Kenyan doctor working for the Ministry of Health. The MVP brought Biko here to Siaya district in October 2004, where he was supposed to divide his time between Sauri's clinic and the government hospital. The MVP website lists the handsome young doctor as one of the experts in Sauri, showcasing his work with the sick, performing C-sections and amputations and ministering to those stricken with

HIV/Aids. But villagers say that after several months, Biko abruptly stopped coming to Sauri. It has been reported that he quit after discovering that a new wing of the Sauri clinic was, in his words, "a ghastly unstable mound of bricks". When I asked Biko why he left, he refused to reply, saying only that his answer might hurt Sachs, who wasn't to blame.

Government employees like Biko are crucial to the MVP's long-term viability, because the future process of "scaling up" from the research sites to fully functioning villages throughout Kenya and elsewhere will fall to government. As Sachs and the MVP envision it, the $110 per person annual contribution – roughly $550,000 per village, or $1.9 billion a year for the 17 million living in extreme poverty in Kenya alone – will be divided between non-governmental organisations and wealthy countries[1], which will supply about 64 per cent, the remainder coming from the host countries and villagers, at least partially in the form of doctors, administrators and agronomists. Whether this financial structure is viable remains to be seen. For example, at the time of the VIP tour, Kenya had provided just five employees, including Biko.

After the hospital tour, the donors were driven a short distance to a dirt road paralleling a defunct railroad track and small plots of crops. A short hike along a narrow footpath in order to glimpse the fields and the fallows was planned, but before we began, Sachs called everyone to attention. He wanted to explain why we had visited the hospital, perhaps to allay any confusion for donors expecting to see only examples of the project's success. The hospital tour, he said, was meant to demonstrate that "you weren't seeing the fruits of the project yet. You're seeing the needs." Just then, a green SUV with tinted windows pulled up beside us. From it stepped a dapper middle-aged man in a suit and tie who strode into the centre of the circle of visitors. "How is everybody?" he asked, smiling. "I'm a bit late because I didn't get the programme. So I've been running around, and fortunately I've been able to meet you. But welcome, and I will join the programme."

Such was the arrival of Jakoyo Midiwo, Siaya district

member of parliament, local restaurant owner, and barroom brawler – and, judging from the sheepish expression on Patrick Mutuo's face, someone who had not been invited on the tour. Now that he was here, Midiwo could hardly be sent packing, and he joined the group as if he belonged.

"Most hated village"

I had already met Midiwo several days earlier, at his stylish restaurant-bar in Kisumu, where he treated me to a round of Tusker, a local beer. Midiwo told me he was a supporter of the MVP, albeit with reservations, ones he would have liked to discuss with the project's leaders. His primary complaint involved the dispersal of money in Sauri to the exclusion of the other locations within the district.

"Sauri is the upmarket part of my constituency, and now they're taking it to a place that is even better," Midiwo had told me, taking a swallow from his third beer. "I would want to take that money to the poorest of the poor. There is animosity on the ground. You see, Sauri now is the most hated village in my constituency. People are envious, some are jealous. Got to start with the neediest first."

The problem, according to Midiwo, was not just where the MVP funds were spent but how. For example, if the MVP encouraged local farmers to raise cotton, Midiwo believed his district would be better positioned to exploit foreign investment incentives like the U.S. African Growth and Opportunities Act of 2000, which lowers trade barriers to sub-Saharan African countries that export textile products, such as cotton T-shirts, to the United States. There is significant potential for economic gain by substituting or augmenting maize with cotton, which, until its collapse here in the early nineties, was the basis of a promising industry in Kenya. According to a 1998 study on farming choices in Siaya district published in the *American Journal of Agricultural Economics*, small-scale Kenyan farmers could earn a third more per hectare by favouring cotton production over maize.

We left the roadside via a narrow dirt road made uneven by water erosion. Most of the donors kept their eyes on the ground, gingerly picking their way through the crop fields. The trail led to a gently sloping hillside that we learned had only recently been dug up and graded to protect a nearby spring from contamination by sewage runoff. At the spring, a series of footpaths converged near a stand of tall green maize stalks. In the distance, I could see small groupings of tin-roofed homesteads, each protectively encircled by trees and shrubs. A dozen women and men from the MVP water and executive committee stood in a semicircle above the spring, waiting expectantly for us to arrive. When we all had gathered, they broke into a traditional Luo song in praise of Sanchez and Sachs, the women and men clapping a slow beat and swaying rhythmically under the sweltering sun. One man held aloft a hand-drawn blue poster that read, SAURI WATER AND SANITATION DEPARTMENT. MOTTO: WATER IS LIFE.

The VIPs watched distractedly, some chatting quietly while others fiddled with their digital cameras, snapping a few photos. When the song was over, the water-committee members explained that the MVP had taught them how to build a large underground tank to protect the spring water, which would then flow year-round out of a spigot protruding from a smooth wall on the hillside. Previously, one woman said, they had filled their buckets cup by cup, but now the spring flowed like tap water. To demonstrate, village women walked down the curve of new red clay steps and took turns at the spigot. Each filled a large plastic bucket with water, hoisted it atop her head, and then performed an impressively nimble balancing act with a single hand as she ascended the stairs.

Simple as this small demonstration of water management may seem, it actually represents what Sachs, in an interview I conducted with him in New York after my trip to Sauri, called "one of the great challenges, in general. Not only in Sauri but throughout Africa." The World Health Organisation estimates that 288 million people in sub-Saharan Africa lack access to reliably clean water and that another 437 million do not have adequate sanitation systems. "There are many approaches to water management in rain-fed agriculture," Sachs explained, ticking off a series of progressive options like farm ponds for irrigation, landscapes and structures for harvesting rainwater, drought-tolerant crops, even insurance that allows farmers to recoup their investments when the rains fail. "We will do all of them in some way," he said.

"Escaping poverty is hard work"

In Sauri, the impact of such wide-ranging ambition can be readily felt. Two years ago, for example, the MVP conducted a series of tests to assess the contamination threats to the local water supply. The results showed that less than half of the twenty local springs considered safe for drinking from actually were. In response, the MVP recommended that the water and sanitation committees repair eleven water tanks and organise the construction of four new boreholes. For all building projects, the MVP requires the relevant committees to first submit a project proposal. The villages then supply the labour and a portion of the necessary materials. It is a seemingly reasonable exchange but one that demonstrates the ways in which the MVP's idealism careers headlong into the realities of survival. Each day, the residents of Sauri must see to their farms, haul water, make repairs to their homesteads and any equipment, care for their children, prepare food over a fire, and wash their clothes by hand. This heavy schedule leaves little surplus time to meet the demands of the MVP's bureaucratic development style, which entails weekly meetings of Sauri's 108 MVP committees. I spoke with several members of one of the twelve water committees, and a number of them expressed unhappiness about the amount of time the meetings required. One woman, a widowed mother of seven, told me she devoted ten full days during the all-important harvest to digging and pouring cement for a water-storage tank. She said she often worked four days a week on the springs – collecting money from her neighbours, organising volunteers, and attending meetings.

When asked if perhaps the MVP was placing too great of a time burden on the Sauri villagers, Sachs told me, "All of these strains are real, but they're hardly unique to life." He said that the MVP is less concerned with day-to-day issues than with "finding pathways for impoverished people out of extreme poverty". He also knows that the small MVP resident staff is stretched thin, but he's determined to keep costs in Sauri as low as possible and points out that "escaping poverty is hard work".

After the spring, the VIPs were taken to see a Sauri homestead, where Okech introduced them to a shy young woman outside a brand-new mud hut with a corrugated tin roof. She stood, arms twisted in front of her, as Okech explained that the woman had recently lost her husband. In traditional Luo society, widows rely on the practice of wife inheritance – a *de facto* welfare system in which women automatically become an additional wife to a surviving brother-in-law – to ensure a minimum level of financial support. (Wife inheritance has diminished in Luo culture since the onset of HIV/Aids.) Even if a woman is inherited, she remains a second-class citizen in the eyes of most Luo, a circumstance Okech, the second wife in a polygamous marriage, knew only too well. Luo tradition requires women to plant or harvest crops depending on their position in the marital hierarchy, beginning with the primary wife and working downward. Subordinate wives run the risk of planting or harvesting their crops late or not at all if a superior wife falls behind in her farm work. Okech escaped this cultural bind when she became the owner of a dairy cow donated to her by a World Bank official. Now, even if her crops are delayed, she still has milk to sell, a source of great pride to her. "My husband would offer me money," she said, "but it was only pocket change."

The widow Okech introduced us to had remained unmarried, and because she received no financial support from either her fellow villagers or the Kenyan government, she had lapsed into abject poverty. Her hut had grown so dangerously dilapidated that her small store of maize was jeopardised. Okech had proposed to Sanchez that the MVP supply corrugated tin sheets and roofing nails for a new house, and promised that the widow would donate any necessary materials, plus labour. Okech expanded the project to include other widows in Sauri, who, again largely because of HIV/Aids, made up 33 per cent of adult village women.

"We organised ourselves through the executive, and we've already put up 38 such houses," Okech told the VIPs, who, seemingly recovered from their languor at the spring, clapped with enthusiasm. But Okech believed that the new houses, much like the reliance on subsistence maize farming, were insufficient. What the women really needed was a reliable income. "We would also love them to have something like dairy cows," she told the VIPs. "This is part of trying to get rid of hunger in Sauri." At the words "get rid of hunger", Sanchez awkwardly called out, "All right!" eliciting another burst of applause from the donors. Mutuo immediately announced that the group was running late and began anxiously ushering everyone to the next presentation. As we left, the wife of the Japanese diplomat to the UN said to me, "That widow was very attractive. She won't be single for long."

More good news
Our final stop brought us to Konjra, a village near Sauri that was designated to be home to one of the upcoming Millennium II locations. About 300 villagers had assembled in a clearing next to a field of cassava and potato plants to hear Sachs, Sanchez, and other dignitaries deliver inspirational speeches about the MVP. The Konjra villagers were seated on the ground, fanned out in a circle around a clump of tall trees next to which the speakers stood, while the donors settled into plastic folding chairs. Low clouds on the horizon moved in, blocking the brilliant rays of sunlight and providing welcome relief from the long day's intense heat.

"We have spent the day so far in the Millennium Type I, Sauri sub-location," Sanchez began. "Thanks to the generosity of many people, some of them who are present here, the Millennium Project is now able to expand from one sub-location to ten." He paused, waiting for his words to be translated into Luo. "The success of Sauri," he said, a note of passion rising in his voice, "has energised the world."

The crowd responded with loud applause and great whoops of joy. Sanchez quieted them with the promise of more good news: "Thanks to the combination of the great generosity of the government of Japan and of private philanthropists, many of whom are present with us, now this project is expanding to 112 villages in 10 countries in Africa."[2] Like believers at a revival, the listeners went wild.

The Type II sites will receive the same development-aid package as Sauri and the other research villages, although their progress will only be monitored by the MVP, not studied. Following that, the MVP has preliminary plans to establish Type III villages, which will receive training, fund-raising assistance, and manuals, all based on the results found in the research and Type II villages. Another step includes the Millennium Cities Initiative, which is already operational in seven mid-size cities across sub-Saharan Africa, including Kisumu. The Cities programme is designed to foster business relationships with the Millennium Villages; they will also receive instruction from the Earth Institute on how to pursue foreign investment.

Each step of this progression rests on the assumption that what happened in Sauri was not only effective in terms of specific projects – many of which have already been reliably proven in other studies – but also innovative and unprecedented as a full-scale development model. The crucial issue in Sauri, then, is not the lunch programmes or the farming interventions but whether the entire MVP approach, not just to aid but to community involvement and government engagement, actually works.

Which makes the disagreements over whether to distribute the maize surplus and the complaints about tiresome committee meetings even more troubling. As for the government, as long as Sauri remains the subject of popular documentaries, speeches to the United Nations, and reports in international newspapers, it will most likely continue to receive official Kenyan support. Will this still be the case in the coming years, when the global community has moved on to other places and other causes, and when the Kenyan government will be expected to fully meet its fiscal obligations to the project? That's hard to predict.

Money, of course, remains a crucial – and uncertain – factor. Under the $110 per person plan, the MVP is expected to meet 45 per cent of the project's costs, the host government 27 per cent, and villages another 9 per cent, with the rest coming from NGOs. The MVP's detailed accounting of the 2005 fiscal year showed a significant shortfall at each level of the cost-sharing arrangement; the MVP was forced to fund a full 71 per cent of Sauri's total expenses; the Kenyan government covered only 13 per cent, mostly in the form of on-loan extension workers like Steven Biko; the villagers were able to contribute just 6 per cent.

One step at a time

Everything grew quite still when Sachs began to speak. I could hear the slight whip of the wind as the clouds above began to threaten. The audience responded warmly to his remarks, and Sachs became increasingly animated, his voice rising in force and vitality, almost like a cheerleader at a pep rally.

"What are the goals?" he cried. "To fight hunger. To fight poverty. To fight malaria. To fight Aids. To make sure mothers are safe in childbirth. To make sure young children can grow up healthy and go to school, boys and girls. To make sure everybody can have safe water to drink." The VIPs and the villagers were roused to even greater paroxysms of applause; one woman bellowed a long ululation, to which Sachs responded with a guttural "Yesss!" Sachs punctuated his statements to the Konjra villagers about feeding their children, reaping giant harvests, combating Aids and malaria, and taking the "big steps forward" out of poverty with questions. "How does that sound?" he asked. The answer, of course, was an enthusiastic affirmation.

Sachs and the Millennium Villages Project will press forward, in Konjra and elsewhere, despite the limited scientific information and the financial failures, in large part because the results in Sauri, successful or otherwise, are not what the MVP is about. In the *End of Poverty*, Sachs states this notion most clearly: "the world is filled with pilot programmes showing that one intervention or another has proven successful time and again...The main challenge now is not to show what works in a single village or district – though these lessons can be of great importance when novel approaches are demonstrated – but rather to scale up what works to encompass a whole country and even the world." In this light, then, Sauri represents not so much a test case or an opportunity to better understand poverty eradication but is merely a symbol of the promise its end inhabits.

From the nearly black clouds overhead, pinpricks of rain began to fall. Sachs told the villagers how glad he would be to inform Kofi Annan that a new Millennium Village would take root on this very spot. "Let me wish you a happy and healthy new year, and a year of big achievements...thank you for being our partners."

With that, he returned with the VIPs to their cars to begin the long drive to the hotel in Kisumu, where cocktails and dinner were scheduled to begin shortly. The villagers slowly began to make their way home just as the sky cracked open, the rain tumbling earthward in drenching sheets.[3]

Notes

[1] For the time being, however, the MVP will pay the international donors' share of the expenses, in order to demonstrate the value of the model.

[2] The decision to go forward was being made well before a thorough examination of the interventions underway in Sauri – a flagship research village – could be completed. Now, more than a year after Sanchez's announcement, the MVP knows that the free-lunch programme correlated with greatly improved attendance and test scores and that blood tests for malaria decrease costs by accurately identifying those who need treatment; then there was the 150 per cent increase in maize yield. These findings, however, make up only a small percentage of the ongoing programmes in Sauri. The outcomes of the micro-credit, crop-diversification, anti-soil-erosion, and sanitation programmes, as well as others, are still pending. Even so, Sachs declared Sauri and the MVP model a success, predicting that "what happened in this village can happen in the next village and the next village. It can happen all over Africa."

[3] The author has dedicated this article to the late John Onyango, a reporter with Kenya's *Daily Nation* newspaper, who contributed to the reporting of this story.

2

DANCING TO THE DONOR'S TUNE

Bantu Mwaura

I n the past few years, it has become increasingly rare to see new creative works emerging from Kenya's theatre circles in the form of new plays, new productions, or even new ideas.

This is not to say that theatre activity in the country has died down. Most of the activity that drives theatre in Kenya today can be categorised into three broad types: "textbook dramas" that have become the main attraction at the Kenya National Theatre (KNT) in Nairobi; British farces that have become the bane of local creativity and which have become regular features at various theatre spaces in the country; and a third rapidly growing type of theatre, which I call "NGO theatre" – the so-called community theatre that is being practised by a large number of artists within the non-governmental sector and whose focus is the dissemination of information on development issues.

The textbook dramas are generally conveyor-belt plays churned out by mercenary-type cartels that produce plays based on text books that form part of the secondary school curriculum. Very little creativity goes into the productions as the amateur actors engage in mere recital of lines, without providing any interpretive approach to the plays that they perform. They nevertheless continue to enjoy captive audiences in the form of students, who, for some inexplicable reason, continue to fill theatre houses even when it is clear that the productions are way below acceptable standards.

The other kind of theatre productions that attract a keen audience are comedies, most of which are British bedroom farces, that, like the textbook dramas, take the cheap route to attract ticket sales – in this case, the use of sexually banal images and suggestive language. While there is nothing wrong with doing bedroom farces, British or not, the one conspicuous aspect of these productions is that they are poorly produced with unimaginably pitiable standards of acting. And if the adult public has continued to watch them, it is because, really, they are provided with no other choice, since the only other theatre activity that seems to be thriving in Kenya is theatre produced by non-governmental organisations (NGOs) – which some have even dubbed as "Aids-driven theatre", given its propensity to produce dull and predictable plays or musicals with a strong HIV/Aids theme.

The theatre driven by the NGO sector in Kenya is single-mindedly concerned with the specific development issues that seem to animate the donor community at any given time. In recent years, no issue seems to have touched the donors more than that of Aids. Ever since HIV/Aids emerged as a continental crisis in the 1990s, the donor community has – in Kenyan political parlance – "poured money" into NGOs that are given the task of sensitising the Kenyan public on matters related to the disease. The result is that theatre activities that claim to be using "theatre for development" as a methodology to disseminate development information to the community have mushroomed. This NGO- and donor-driven theatre differs from the other two forms of theatre (that is, the textbook dramas and the bedroom farces) in one other way: it has attracted a lot of artistes because of the quick and easy money that can be made. Actors, producers, playwrights and directors who might have spent their time in engaging in creative works of their own are now acting, producing, writing and directing plays that not only have little entertainment value, but which are dictated to them by donor-funded NGOs.

The development trap
How did we get to this point? History gives us some pointers.

Part of the structural challenge of development in post-colonial Africa is that soon after independence, African leaders proclaimed a development ideology that did not necessarily translate into a programme of societal transformation, simply because they were more interested in raw power and self-aggrandisement. As such, they were consumed by the destructive politics of survival. This scenario provided an excuse for both the former colonial masters and the leaders of the newly independent nations to justify the push for a development paradigm that continued the imperialist/colonial practice of trashing indigenous processes, however progressive, and basing African development on Western modernisation.

The modernisation project led to the destruction of many traditional values and practices, which were deemed "uncivilised" and "backward" by none other than the Africans themselves. Cultural practices that once held communities together and gave meaning to their lives were eroded to give way to practices and ideas that were not only alien, but in some cases, detrimental to post-colonial African societies.

For instance, traditional Kenyan communities, like those in other parts of Africa, have cultural practices coded in elaborate performance forms that are as theatrical as they are communal. The nature of indigenous performance forms, including song, dance, poetry and storytelling, were essentially participatory in nature. Unlike classical Western theatre, where the line between the performers and the audience is clearly drawn, in African forms of theatre, the performers and the audience are often one and the same – both participate in the performance. These performances were also a means of imparting important information on expected norms and behaviour to the community, for example to adolescents during coming-of-age ceremonies. Their participatory nature also ensured communal unity, the very aspect of social organisation that the colonialists sought to annihilate.

These participatory theatrical and cultural practices were destroyed by the colonial project of "civilising" indigenous communities, since those very practices were viewed by the colonialists as primitive and bordering on witchcraft. Many of these performance and cultural practices were subsequently banned by the colonialists. With respect to theatre, for example, the Western institution of repertory theatre was introduced at various levels. Together with the practice that saw several "little theatres" built in major emerging urban centres, the idea of repertory theatre was introduced in the school system, where the students were normally trained in classical Shakespearean theatre styles, a trend that continues to this day.

However, with the advent of multiparty politics across Africa and the opening up of democratic space in the 1990s, it became fashionable for donors to advocate for people-based approaches that included development communication strategies that are participatory in nature. In Kenya, this gave rise to a flurry of activities in "development communication" – a concept that was popularised in the latter half of the 20th century, and which is concerned mainly with the role of communication in bringing about social transformation.

The aim of development communication is to increase community participation through the use of both interpersonal and mass media as a way of achieving self-reliance and empowerment. It is this thinking that saw an increase in the activity of civil societies across Africa. In Kenya, this period (from the late 1980s through much of the 1990s) saw an increase in the registration of non-governmental organisations (NGOs), whose main focus was the dissemination of important development information deemed crucial to the process of social change, including issues related to civic education, HIV/Aids and domestic violence. Unfortunately, the target communities remained mere spectators in a process that was led mainly by donors and NGOs, not the communities themselves.

Act One : The first phase of theatre for development
The process of social transformation demands a communication strategy that ensures self-reliance and one that utilises participatory methods. This means that the target community has to be involved in defining its own problems and designing strategies to deal with their own challenges. One such communication strategy that has

immense and unequalled potential in its a ability to be truly participatory is theatre, particularly the methods that have been developed over time and which are now invariably referred to as Theatre for Development (TfD), Community Theatre, and Participatory Educational Theatre (PET), which are basically variations of the same.

What TfD and similar approaches have done is to amplify the techniques that target attitude and behaviour change and make them more efficient.[1] The TfD methodology is one that consciously allows the people in a community to use theatrical techniques to explore their own problems and challenges and thereby engage in the process of self-education. Its main aim is to craft messages from available information in such a way that allows the audience to actively participate in the analysis of social problems and in the search for solutions, a process that allows the participants to achieve attitude change since the process of raising consciousness is affirmed by active participation.[2]

As opposed to other forms of media, TfD's efficiency as a development communication strategy – by virtue of being a live medium – allows for information to be configured to fit specific situations and to accommodate socio-cultural differences, while responding to specific and immediate challenges in ways that neither the electronic nor the print media are able to do.

The 1990s saw the re-emergence of TfD practice in Kenya – I call it a "re-emergence" because, as some critics have argued, the practice of TfD in Kenya can be divided into two phases. The first phase can roughly be considered as the pre-1990 period, the highlight of which was the work done by, among others, author and playwright Ngugi wa Thiong'o and his collaborators at the famous Kamiriithu Educational and Cultural Centre in Limuru, where rural communities formed an integral part of the production process. Unfortunately, this kind of theatre was quashed by the regimes of presidents Jomo Kenyatta and Daniel arap Moi because of its implicit and explicit messages of empowerment and self-reliance, two concepts that the two leaders were apparently averse to.

By the late 1980s, this kind of theatre practice in Kenya had been suppressed to the level where no plays could be presented without state censorship. Not even the Kenya Schools and Colleges Drama Festival was spared the censorship that was visited upon artists, writers and intellectuals by the state, a situation that resulted in the festival becoming a training ground for political sycophants – comprising both fawning students and teachers – as schools endeavoured to outdo each other in producing plays, songs and dances that were nothing more than sugar-coated odes in praise of the sitting president.

This period also saw the works of numerous artists and university academics proscribed, and eventually led Ngugi wa Thiong'o to flee the country after he was detained without trial for engaging in "activities and utterances which are dangerous to the good Government of Kenya and its institutions".[3] More specifically, the TfD work that Ngugi wa Thiong'o was doing in Limuru with the local people at the Kamiriithu Cultural and Educational Centre was banned and the Kamiriithu Theatre razed to the ground. (Later, a village polytechnic was built by the government at the very place where the makeshift theatre stood, clearly as a way of erasing the memory of the participatory theatre work done by the villagers under the direction of Ngugi wa Thiong'o.) The physical destruction of the Kamiriithu Centre was technically the death of community-based theatre in Kenya.

It was not until the 1990s, after heightened political agitation and international pressure, that the Moi regime relented and allowed the re-emergence of community-based theatre in the country. [4] However, this did not mean that the government actively supported the development of community or any other kind of theatre in the country, with the result that the Kenya National Theatre – which was under the direct control of the government – became a popular venue for holding private weddings and prayer meetings, mainly because private individuals and evangelists were the only ones who could afford to hire the theatre hall. (Many of Nairobi's once-grand cinema halls, such as the Odeon and the Globe, are today hired for the same reasons every weekend.) Because the government does not provide funding to support theatre and cultural activities, foreign cultural missions or the cultural arms of foreign governments have taken advantage of the vacuum to push their own agendas by providing funding and sponsorship for theatrical performances.

Local artists and theatre practitioners who have not been fortunate enough to access funding from other sources to support their work have sought innovative ways in which to ensure a continued engagement with theatre. A good example is the emergence in the 1990s of what has been termed as "bar theatre" – a practice that saw popular plays performed in restaurants and pubs across the country. This form of theatre was motivated by the realisation that many potential theatre-goers in Kenya spent large amounts of their leisure time in bars. It was a case of "if they cannot come to the theatre, the theatre will go to them". This practice was perfected by the late Wahome Mutahi, a much-loved humour columnist and playwright who never missed an opportunity to parody the political class in the country both in his weekly column titled *Whispers* and in his plays written in the Gikuyu language. The "bar theatre" is an important phenomenon in the history of Kenyan theatre practice because for the first time the country witnessed long- running local productions. Mutahi's *Mugaathe Mubogothi,* loosely translated as "His Excellency the Delirious", for example, had a two-year run with performances taking place in bars and restaurants every weekend. These productions were entirely supported by box office sales.

Act Two: Enter the NGOs

During this period, the nature and purpose of community-based theatre had also changed. The registration and the work of civil society organisations and NGOs increased manifold, and since most of them justified their existence by working with and in the communities, it was not long before they discovered the latent power of using TfD in their community-related projects. Their activities constitute the second phase of TfD practice in the post-1990 period.

The movement that saw organisations within civil society in the early 1990s increasingly employ Participatory Rural Appraisal (PRA) methods in their development communication strategies benefited greatly from the work that was being done by theatre artists who were committed to using indigenous methods of participatory theatre in their general work as thespians. Of prominence is the Theatre Workshop Productions (TWP) – a theatre company carved out of the University of Nairobi's Free Travelling Theatre and whose work progressively moved from the Free Travelling Theatre tradition, where the department of literature at the University of Nairobi would tour play productions all over the country in community theatre projects.

The travelling theatre movement emerged in various parts of Africa as a way of negating the colonially-imposed practice of presenting classical European plays modelled on the London West End repertory theatre tradition. This movement emerged within institutions of higher learning based in urban centres with the aim of presenting popular drama to the general public, particularly in rural areas, and also as a way of recuperating indigenous pre-colonial performance traditions. The travelling theatre movement made conscious efforts to adapt participatory and popular performance forms, thereby moving away from the ivory tower construct of the universities and into the practice of community theatre proper.[5]

It is the work that members of TWP pioneered in the development communication sector that forms the early period of the second phase of TfD practice in Kenya, which is also marked by the increased involvement of NGOs. In this second phase, a cross-section of issues that demanded the interventions of development communication mushroomed almost overnight and many NGOs took advantage of showcase community theatre work that had been done by the likes of TWP. Legal and human rights NGOs began using theatre to sensitise the public on relevant human rights and constitutional issues.

Similarly, a myriad other organisations used theatre to communicate HIV/Aids issues. The story of HIV/Aids and theatre is most telling since there has been a great commitment by the donor community to focus on HIV/Aids. Yet there is no comprehensive or widely available method of monitoring and evaluating the use of TfD to raise awareness about HIV/Aids or community health. No substantive evaluation has been developed locally to monitor the use of TfD or to measure its impact on attitude and behaviour change beyond internal organisational reports and statistics on the unprecedented rise in condom sales in the country.

Clearly, the striking difference between the first and the second phases of the TfD practice in Kenya lies in the fact that this second phase has seen a TfD practice that enjoys funding from both local NGOs and international donor organisations, yet it is the phase that has furnished the circumstances that have ensured the underdevelopment of TfD in the country.

It is curious that the emergence of what I refer to as "NGO theatre" – as opposed to TfD – saw the collapse of well-established theatre groups, such as Mbalamwezi Players, Friends Theatre, Chelepe Arts, Mzizi Creative Centre, among others, which had established themselves as progressive breeding grounds for new theatrical productions and for the informal training of theatre practitioners as actors, directors and producers. These groups managed to carry out their work over a long period of time without any substantive support from any quarters – even the government, as is the practice all over the world – and only survived through ingenious commercial approaches to theatre practice. To a large extent, most of these groups relied on box office earnings and occasional sponsorships from the corporate world.

When the development sector turned to and increased the demand for the use of theatre in their communication strategies, it certainly was seen as a godsend by many artistes since now, at an individual level, they could consult for NGOs and development agencies and earn relatively higher wages than they could ever hope to earn by merely practising theatre independently.[6] This scenario gave rise to two profoundly disturbing phenomena: one, it resulted in the death of independent theatre groups; and two, since a lot of NGOs were getting onto the TfD bandwagon, any artist with any slight pretensions to TfD knowledge was sucked into NGO theatre.

NGO theatre, or the NGO-fication of theatre practice in Kenya, itself resulted in two directly connected phenomena: one, the process gave rise to a theatre practice that was entirely funded by donor agencies and NGOs, both local and international; and two, and most importantly, it was a type of theatre practice that emerged from the anomaly resulting from a demand for TfD practice without corresponding expertise in the same.

NGO theatre is therefore about middlemen and women who engage in development brokerage with two groups – the NGOs that get financial support in the name of community development and the so-called theatre practitioners who claim to be engaging in theatre for development even when they clearly have questionable training even in basic theatre.

In other words, NGO theatre can be seen as a coin with two sides; one side being the practice of community theatre without the community and the other side being the practice of theatre for development without the development.

Notes

[1] Zakes Mda's *When People Play People: Development Communication Through Theatre*, (1993) is roundly illustrative of the workings of theatre as a method in development communication in Africa, with specific case studies from Southern Africa.

[2] This process of conscientisation is well elaborated by Paulo Freire's idea of participatory approaches to the problem-solving pedagogy in education in his seminal work *Pedagogy of the Oppressed*. This is the same theoretical approach that Augusto Boal has used to espouse his methodology of *Forum Theatre* in his TfD work well captured in his ground breaking book under the title *Theatre of the Oppressed*.

[3] Detention order dated 29 December 1977.

[4] A detailed study of the Kamiriithu Theatre can be found in Ingrid Bjorkman's book *Mother Sing for Me: People's Theatre in Kenya* 1989.

[5] David Kerr's book *African Popular Theatre* (1995) gives a good account of the emergence of the Free Travelling Theatre in Africa

[6] Indeed, in a study carried out by C.J. Odhiambo, a senior lecturer at Moi University and published in *Research in Drama Education* (2005) interrogating the ethics of TfD practice in Kenya, Odhiambo refers to candid responses from informants – themselves TfD practitioners – who clearly indicate that they are in it merely because "it is an avenue for employment" and in any case "there was too much money from donors literally chasing TfD projects dealing with the so-called "burning issues", that is HIV/Aids, female genital mutilation (FGM), civic education, conflict resolution… among others." It is largely agreed that a good bit of the work that is touted as TfD and financially underwritten by a good number of NGOs in Kenya today has little or nothing to do with community development; it is rather engaging in community theatre in name or at best community theatre without the community. Like Odhiambo, Lenin Ogolla in his book *Towards Behaviour Change: Participatory Education and Development* (1997) laments about the ethical problems facing TfD practice in Kenya and states that while many development workers and NGOs "have a fair sense of the power of drama and theatre," it is clear that "their relative lack of expertise in this field makes them gullible to any professional idlers who prefer to call

themselves thespians." He further grieves that the civic education movement in Kenya, for example, "has created several opportunities for quacks who want to turn the fight for democracy into an industry."

3

THE MAASAI INVASIONS

Parselelo Kantai

Friday, the 13th of August 2004, dawned grey with the threat of end-of-the-week downtown Nairobi chaos. The streets were thick snails of traffic. The sidewalks flowed not much faster, viscous with humanity, a slow-moving riot of colour. Even at this hour, the pretty college girls stood out in the crowd, already dressed up for Friday night clubbing. The whole of Nairobi seemed to gather on the city streets: job-seekers, vegetable hawkers, trinket traders, street-preachers, thieves.

It was not a day prepared for riots. And yet the promise of a riot, of some police action or another, loomed large. The Maasai were demonstrating. By mid-morning about 300 men and women from the Maasai community, distinctive in their red and blue *shukas*[1], had gathered on the grounds of the Kenyatta International Conference Centre (KICC), Nairobi's emblematic 28-storey-high building, the pride of the city's rising skyline. The Maasai demonstrators stood around in little groups. Reporters from the local and international press flitted from group to group looking for anyone who could provide background info – several impromptu interviews were occurring simultaneously. Some reporters gathered around the twin figures of Maa Civil Society Forum chairman Ben ole Koissabba, a logistics officer with World Vision International, the Christian charity, and Sidney Quntai, a former journalist now running an NGO called the Human-Wildlife Conflict Network.

I could not see Elijah Marima ole Sempeta. Tall and light-skinned, he always stood out in a crowd. He was a young, outspoken and brash Maasai lawyer who had made headlines in early 2003 by demanding back-royalties from the Magadi Soda Company, a mining company that had been extracting soda ash from Lake Magadi since 1911. Located in the old Southern Province (which contained the two Maasai districts of Narok and Kajiado), Magadi Soda produces almost 40 per cent of global soda output. In 2004, the parent company was wholly British.[2] (It has since been acquired by the Indian conglomerate, the Tata Group.) The original company, Brunner, Mond & Co., was founded in Northwich, England, by Ludwig Mond. Magadi was the company's most profitable soda ash operation.[3] Soda ash is used in the manufacture of glass and paper and in the bleaching industry. Royalties from the Company's operation had always been paid to the central government. Sempeta argued that Lake Magadi, and the thousands of acres that had been ceded to the Company by the colonial government, had been illegally "grabbed" from the Maasai. And the Maasai had received nothing by way of compensation.

The agitation for compensation coincided with the Magadi Soda Company's negotiations with the International Finance Company (IFC), the World Bank's private sector lending arm, for a $100 million loan facility. The Magadi-IFC negotiations were almost complete. All that remained was an environmental audit and an assurance that their lease would be extended when it expired in 2023. Sempeta led a highly-publicised demonstration accusing the Company of abuses against the Maasai, taking demonstrators on a 40-km walk from baking-hot Magadi into Nairobi and addressing the media in tones that were sure to alarm the visiting IFC delegation. The demonstration stunned the Company, which had considered this final stage of the negotiations a mere formality. The police were brought in. According to Magadi residents I interviewed around the time of the campaign, anybody known or suspected of being associated with the demonstration was arrested. Police harassment continued for weeks afterwards. Although the loan was granted in the end, Sempeta's name was now on the map. He, along with the likes of ole Koissabba, was considered by many to be the inspiration behind the August 13th demonstration.

At KICC, all the local dailies had reporters present. There were also TV crews from the Kenya Television Network (KTN) and Reuters. Demonstrators handed around placards, others scribbled slogans on manila paper. Several carried yet other placards with slogans like: "We Demand Our Land Back From the British!" and "100 Years Is Enough!" and "The Laikipia Leases Have Expired Give the Maasai Back Their Land!" Journalists were informed that there would be similar demonstrations in four other towns – Kajiado, Naivasha, Nanyuki and Narok, all located in what can be called Maasailand – and all would begin at the same time.

The demonstrations had originally been planned for the 15th of August 2004, a date that marked the centenary of the signing of the first Anglo-Maasai Agreement under which the Maasai had, so the Agreement states, "willingly" ceded their territory in the Central Rift Valley to move to two reserves, one to the north of the newly constructed Kenya-Uganda Railway, and the other to the south of it. (The Agreement, the Maasai were assured, would last "as long as the Maasai still exist as a race".) But because August 15th fell on a Sunday, the organisers, a pressure group called the Maa Civil Society Forum (MCSF), had moved the demonstrations forward to Friday the 13th. Sunday is a slow news day in Kenya; people go to church.

The media was central to the campaign strategy: Maasai claims for the resolution of outstanding grievances had always been made behind closed doors, and addressed directly to the State. This particular campaign would in fact be the fourth time over the past century that the Maasai would be challenging the loss of their lands. All three previous attempts – a court case in 1913, a petition in 1932 to the Kenya Land Commission and a plea made at the Kenya Constitutional Conference in London in 1962 on the eve of Kenya's independence – ended in bitter failure. Exposing the issue to public scrutiny would have the calculated aim of embarrassing a popularly elected government and thus forcing it to negotiate. While the campaign's broad objective was land restitution, the initial focus was on the return of Laikipia, the two-million-acre site of the former northern Maasai Reserve, home to a handful of white ranchers, mostly descendants of the white settler community. The 13th August demonstration was planned as part of a series that would culminate in the presentation of a petition to the Kenyan and British governments demanding the return of lands allegedly stolen from the Maasai during the colonial era, and financial compensation for the trauma of land loss and resultant "under-development" of the Maasai community. By the time the demonstration started, the crowd had doubled.

These demonstrations had been in the works for at least a year. I had been involved with the MCSF since early 2003 during the Magadi campaign when the most recent discussions about agitating for the return of stolen Maasai lands began. The Maa Forum was the brainchild of a group of Maasai professionals – lawyers, journalists and NGO activists. The logic behind the present agitation – there had been three others since 1912 – was that since the Laikipia leases expired on August 15th, the land should revert to the Maasai people. Some 37 white settler families occupied the land. From early 2003, there had been rumours that the Laikipia settlers were worried about the expiry of the leases; with a new government in place, there were no guarantees that their interests would be protected. Stories abounded of panic selling and secret missions by settler lobby groups to the Minister of Lands. I was never able to confirm any of them.

The demonstrators set off. At the front of the procession a chant started; a stirring popular Maasai gospel tune that rippled through the group, became a roar that echoed against the government buildings on both sides of Harambee Avenue. The line of pedestrians on the sidewalks, thinner now without office workers, seemed for a moment to pause, as if zapped by the singing. And then people gathered their wits and warily looked around for the first signs of trouble, sniffed the air for the very teargas of it – for the tell-tale signs of riot police. None appeared. Not yet anyway. Tension gave way to spontaneous conversations among strangers.

The marchers were a mixed bunch underneath the red

and blue of their traditional dress, their beads and bracelets. Many were Maasai from out of town, men and women for whom Nairobi, with its alien noises and rhythms, its exhaust fumes and high-rises, was the concrete jungle. Others wore office clothes underneath the traditional garb. They had the morning off from work in precisely those high-rises, to participate in what they considered a historical moment. I realised this as I fell into step with a woman who was singing soprano, as tears streamed down her cheeks. She smiled as she caught my eye and for a moment I felt a rush of uncontrollable emotion. Where was she from, I asked. Narok, she said, but she worked in a company in the city centre and lived in Kitengela, on the outskirts of the city. Why was she here, I asked. She was half-jogging and half-singing, only part in conversation with me. Now she turned fully to me: How could she *not* be here? Our lands had been stolen and continued to disappear. Our children were growing up without a sense of who they were. She was, she said, playing her part in making a change. Ten days later I would see her on TV, weeping again, as the riot police bludgeoned her.

As we marched, I saw an uncle of mine whom I had not seen in months. He was standing at the junction of Aga Khan Walk and Harambee Avenue waiting for the demonstration to pass, arrested by the spectacle. I stopped and we chatted briefly. He was curious to know what was going on. Here in downtown Nairobi he was more city man in suit and tie than Maasai. He declined my invitation to join the demo, appeared slightly embarrassed by the display of *shukas*, the singing. He had things to do, he said, and quickly crossed the road.

My family is from Ngong in Kajiado, one of the nine districts in Kenya that form Maasailand. My grandfather, Nathaniel Kantai ole Seet, is from the section known as Kaputiei, from the Enkidong'i clan, the clan of *laibons* or spiritual leaders. His father, Seet ole Nagela, was an *olaiguenani* or chief counsellor, who the British too appointed as one of their chiefs. My grandfather moved to Ngong in the 1920s while tending herds of cattle on

European settler farms in the Rift Valley. At his last job, he disagreed with the European farm manager, punched him out and moved permanently to Ngong. It is a story that some of my older uncles like to tell, although they are equally proud of a long wooden table – painted over in a garish green and which is used at family gatherings – that my grandfather received "personally from the *mzungu* owner" as an appreciation for rendering faithful service. My grandfather would continue to tend his herds but he would also adopt Christianity and send his children to school, a rare occurrence in Maasailand in those days. It is a story that contains, in other words, the double-helix of the Maasai relationship with the British: resistance and collaboration.

Press photographers dashed to the front of the singing procession, crouched and snapped away, darted to the other side of the street, trying to capture the Portrait of Fierce Maasai Moran as Political Activist Out of His Element on the Streets of Nairobi and a front-page credit in tomorrow's papers. Down Harambee Avenue the group headed, the chanting incantatory, the demonstrators falling in love with their own baritones. Harambee Avenue: The address of the Office of the President, Justice and Constitutional Affairs and Foreign Affairs – executive authority and national best-foot-forward. State Power.

The Administration Police officers (APs) manning the gates at the Ministry of Justice were polite but firm: they would allow neither the group nor any of its representatives in to deliver the petition they had with them. Entitled *A Memorandum on the Anglo-Maasai Agreements: A Case of Historical and Contemporary Injustices and the Dispossession of Maasai Land*, the petition, addressed to the Kenyan and British governments, makes two demands. The first is the return of Laikipia, the old Northern Reserve:

> The Maa community does strongly urge the Government of Kenya not to extend any of the leases, which are at the verge of expiring. Instead, the land should be reverted back to the Maa community. The land is theirs.[4]

The second is a demand for compensation:

> The Kenyan and British Governments should compensate
> the Maa communities for all the historical and contemporary
> injustices subjected to them. The compensation should be in
> the form of lands and territories equal in quality, size and
> legal status to those taken away from them wrongfully. It
> should also include monies to mitigate their social-cultural
> welfare such as education, livestock management and
> markets, amenities and infrastructure. The compensation
> should be just, prompt and fair to benefit all the population
> of Maa people.[5]

Fifteen minutes of cajoling the APs had produced no
results. The singing had become sporadic, breaking out
from different parts of the procession like an itch on a
sweaty body. Once again people were standing around in
small groups, the procession leaders haranguing and
cajoling the sphinx-like APs, others interviewing and
strategising, and yet others studying the petition once
again. I fell into conversation with a tall man aged about
30. He was dressed in jeans and a T-shirt, and his afro was
fashionably uncombed. He wore a Maasai bracelet on his
wrist, as if to say that he straddled two worlds, a modern
one and a traditional one. He was from Loita in Narok and
had only recently returned from two years in the
Netherlands where he had finished his Masters degree and
was hoping to start work on his doctorate. In between, he
had returned home and was working for a Dutch NGO
that did work among pastoralist communities. There was
about him an air of detachment, as if, like me, he was both
participant and critical observer. He turned to me and
said: "This is our time. We are the warriors now. When our
children ask us what we did for the struggle, we will be able
to tell them about this."

And so the procession was sighing and sweating and
generally catching its collective breath when Assistant
Minister of Justice and Constitutional Affairs, Danson
Mungatana, rolled up to the gate in his brand new official,
white and metallic-silver Toyota Prado. Seeing the TV

cameras and the demonstrators, he realised he had just stumbled on *a situation*. Driving in – sorry, being driven in, he was seated at back-left, waving with the imperial insouciance of a man who has only recently grown accustomed to his new status. Mungatana is a young politician, in his late 30s, who graduated at the top of his law class at the University of Nairobi. Trim and youthful, he is as yet unafflicted by the pot belly, the mark of the political *arriviste*. He is an unlikely defender of the "Mount Kenya Mafia", the Kikuyu-dominated kitchen Cabinet within the NARC[6] coalition widely perceived to be the power behind President Mwai Kibaki. While Mungatana does not have a reputation for corruption, the Mount Kenya Mafia does. He comes from a small, marginalised community at the Coast, the Pokomo, who have land grievances of their own that date back to colonial times.[7] Baby-faced and outspoken, Mungatana often sabotages himself by his eagerness to scrap with "political heavyweights" on behalf of the Mount Kenya Mafia faction. He is said to possess presidential ambitions. And here he finds himself in *a situation*. And it would not do to ignore it and just drive in. For one, it would allow the crowd through the gates and Mungatana had no idea what they wanted. But TV cameras always present an opportunity to make some political mileage in the bickering between the two rival factions within the NARC government. So, reluctantly (although you would never suspect it, the way he made the leap from the back seat of the Prado to the tarmac, the youthful pugnacity of his walk) he gets out of his vehicle and walks directly to the TV cameras, the crowd parting Red Sea-like.

After speaking briefly to the cameras, he accepts the petition, and, switching to Big Man mode proper – a squaring of shoulders and pursing of lips, an elevated gaze into the middle-distance, an extended clearing of the throat – assures the group that the petition "will be studied by the government before a decision is reached".[8] He then walks through the gate, a group of reporters running after him for a quote. Whether he actually delivered the petition to the Justice Minister is another matter altogether; no comment ever emanated from the ministry.

Mungatana was the last public official the Maasai demonstrators would have any contact with, either on that first day of the demonstrations or at any other point during the campaign. The procession left the city centre and snaked one-and-half kilometres up Community Hill to the Ministry of Lands. The Minister, Amos Kimunya, was not in his office, the group was informed. They marched across the road to the British High Commission. Edward Clay, the High Commissioner, was not in either. It was a Friday. The High Commission closed at lunchtime on Fridays. Sempeta and Koissabba refused to hand the petition to young Miss Amanda Rose, the official sacrificed for the occasion. They railed at Clay's unavailability: "Clay's refusal to see us shows how much contempt he has for us. It smacks of colonialism," said Sempeta.[9] One of the placards echoed him: "The British are Equally Gluttonous. Stop Vomiting On Our Ancestral Lands". It was a dig at Clay's recent condemnation of corruption in the Kenya government. He had taken the very undiplomatic but unexpectedly popular position of accusing the government of "being gluttonous" and "vomiting on the shoes of the donors". The public had applauded him. Government officials spluttered their indignation onto the front pages of the dailies.

The police remained quiet that first day, perhaps through no fault of their own. There was nobody *giving* instructions. It was, after all, a Friday in Nairobi. Everybody was lunching, golfing or out-of-towning. They watched and waited.

The petition was delivered to the administration in each of the four towns, with some replays of the Mungatana scenario. For instance in Naivasha, from where the Maasai had been obliged to move in August 1904, exactly a century before, scores of demonstrators reportedly "ambushed" the Rift Valley Provincial Commissioner and presented him with the memorandum. He was, said news reports, preparing to receive President Mwai Kibaki.[10] In Nanyuki, the administrative headquarters of Laikipia district, 3,000 Maasai demonstrated and presented the petition to the District Commissioner as police in riot gear watched from a distance. Everywhere, the demonstrations were said to have been peaceful. Significantly, the media picked up on the issue of the Laikipia leases expiring on August 15th. The lease-expiry issue was to play a crucial role in the future direction of the campaign.

August 15th passed without incident. So far, the campaign had played on two different media registers that were satisfying two different sets of expectations. The local press, which served the literate African middle-class constituency, had presented the campaign as a drama of land dispossession and British colonial injustice, a theme at the heart of the nation's official "liberation struggle" narrative.

However, land dispossession has been distorted in the post-independence era. With the hijacking of anti-colonial struggles by an African nationalist elite that used the rhetoric of African self-determination as a cover for private capital accumulation, it is difficult these days to tell who is worse: the *mzungu* or the *mbenzi*.[11] And so, while the exploitation of public disgust with the nationalist elite has become the standard fare of headline news stories, by casting the Maasai story as a drama whose implications did not necessarily threaten the course of contemporary Kenyan politics, the media was taking its audience on a museum tour. The Maasai story thus opened a window onto the expired relations of another age.

It was as if the public was being primed for a repeat of the last instalment of the Maasai drama with a viewer-friendly ending; justice comes to the African underdog, albeit a century after the crime. In late July and early August of 2004, a two-part series ran in the *Daily Nation* about the Anglo-Maasai treaties.[12] What the nationalists had failed to provide – a closure of the colonial moment – could perhaps be partly offered in this encounter, since the Maasai campaign promised the opportunity to bear witness to one of the last scenes of the colonial drama on terms that, after over 40 years of African rule, seemed to favour the African. In addition, the nature of colonialism could be examined through a lens almost undistorted by the messiness of African elite rule – by the ethnic clientilism, corruption and mismanagement of post-independence nationalist politics. And here was a cast of characters that promised a kind of Galapagos of the theatre of colonialism – petrified early colonial relations between conqueror and conquered suddenly resuscitated, and being contested in contemporary Kenya. A once rich and powerful African people, swindled, dispossessed and impoverished by their encounter with the greedy, hypocritical British colonialist.

The fascination with this drama was enhanced by the location on which the final contest would take place: Laikipia. A faraway place of endless savannahs and rolling mountain ranges teeming with wildlife – less (first Protectorate Commissioner) Eliot's *tabula rasa*,[13] than a huge and finely preserved stage for history's denouement.

Certain details threatened to upset the drama. In late July, President Mwai Kibaki had toured Laikipia District and, in apparent reference to the trauma of the ethnic clashes of the 1990s, assured Kikuyus in the area that they would never be moved from Laikipia against their will.[14] Also, the Minister of Lands and Settlement came from Kipipiri constituency, Laikipia. In the event, the local media followed the campaigners' lead of reconstructing Laikipia as a colonial space existing within a post-colonial environment. It was occupied, not by the mix of Africans, Europeans, pastoralists, peasant farmers, ranchers and *nusu nusus* (mixed race people) who actually lived there, but by "the couple of dozen ethnic European landowners", to paraphrase settler author and Laikipia farmer, Aidan Hartley.[15]

Size was important, central even, to the public's perception of the stated injustice. And the *mzungu* ranch-sizes ranked beyond the dreams of avarice – two million acres owned by 37 families in a country where family feuds over a five-acre piece of land have persisted from one generation to another. *This* Laikipia was, as the Maasai campaigners depicted it, still an occupied zone, still colonised. The basis of this struggle was to wrest it from the "hybrid gluttons...and their heirs".[16] So not only was an old struggle going to be re-enacted, but the ensuing drama would have an added bonus: that the suspects were still at the scene of the crime. Crucially, this "final showdown" promised the audience a rare and blissful opportunity of non-participatory entertainment: the scene had been crafted to carefully avoid the contamination of ethnic competition. The campaigners' strategy of targeting white-owned ranches as an entry-point into a wider land restitution debate ensured an almost guilt-free ride for the audience. By presenting the petition in a colonial context the Maasai had racialised the Laikipia claims without ethnicising them.

Memories of Zim

Whereas the expectations generated for the Kenyan audience by the local press were of restitution and closure, the international audience was sold the story on the strength of fear and racial violence, on the strength, that is, of another story: the Zimbabwe land "invasions". Certain sub-texts were effortlessly and mercilessly exploited: the last white settler under threat from the primitive hordes.[17] The old fear of servant anger. Africa as a series of interconnected villages in which the drum-beats of anti-white land claims resonate deeply from one village to the next, communicating insurrection. And then the invasion, the human equivalent of an African dust storm – unpredictable, sudden. And with domino-like collapse, white communities fall in a bloody scenario of mindless violence.

The Maasai were reconstructed for this purpose. No longer the benign noble savage of an earlier era whose photographs had graced so many coffee-table books, so many tourist postcards, the Maasai moran was re-stereotyped, re-armed, "Mau Mau-ed" – that is, turned into the potential bearer of savagery against Europeans – by virtue of the assumed proximity to the Zimbabwe scenario. He was no longer "inhabiting the vast savannahs of East Africa" but was instead "marching onto sprawling ranches".[18] He was no longer "dressed in traditional regalia" but was "clad in blazing red". And he was no longer "in perfect harmony with nature" but was instead "ready to mount *Zimbabwe-style violence*" on a helpless population of unprotected white settlers.[19]

Later, once the drama in Laikipia was underway, once the story was telling itself, foreign correspondents would stream in. They would leave Nairobi after hurried breakfasts served by grateful, loyal domestic help for $100 a month or less. But not before a quick skim over the local dailies on the porch in Karen or Muthaiga, the old settler suburbs in Nairobi mythologised by Karen Blixen and Elspeth Huxley, and a final round of rapid-fire instructions to the groundsman mowing the lawn that seems to have been designed specifically for their new penchant for endless garden soirees. The way it rolls and slithers and sashays down to the brilliant blue of the swimming pool! And so into the Pajero and off down the long driveway, past the unsmiling armed security at the gate, past the sizzling electric fence – this city wasn't nicknamed Nai-roberry for nothing – and eventually onto Thika Road, north towards Nanyuki. Now, the journalistic nose is hard and jutting. The gaze, having marvelled and raked and imbibed this very scenery over the course of so many holiday weekends, is now sober and fixed behind the RayBans. A gaze not unkind, just...*critical*. The mental notes form and unform, test themselves against the whizzing landscape: delete "endless, undulating plains", replace with "parched African wilderness". It was mostly in response to the foreign media's version of events that the State would respond, would act.

On Saturday, August 21st 2004, a group of Maasai herdsmen cut a section of the Loldaiga Ranch fence in Laikipia and were driving in their herds when a contingent of security personnel from the regular forces as well as the fearsome paramilitary force, the General Service Unit (GSU), arrived and began firing. They were, eye witnesses would later say, accompanied by a white rancher.[20] One herdsman, 70-year old Ntinai ole Moiyare, died on the spot. Three others had serious bullet injuries. Twenty-two spent cartridges were found on the "bloodstained scene". A survivor, said one officer, shot in the air "while the others pointed [their guns] at the herdsmen and shot at them".[21] At Segera Ranch close by, reported the *East African Standard,* a group of Maasai youth, "chanting war songs and armed", charged at a contingent of security officers. The police fired several rounds of ammunition in the air to scare off "the warriors".[22]

With the kind of sloppy self-assurance of the criminal who knows that his alibi is a mere formality in a wider cover-up scheme, the police explained that they had been threatened. The group of herdsmen was armed "with bows, arrows, spears and *rungus* [knob kerries]." A glimpse of what the real transgression had been was found at the end of the statement: "They had cut the barbed wire at one end of the farm."[23] In other words, they had appeared to physically act on the claims made by the August 13th demonstrators.

Another version of the events leading up to the Loldaiga Ranch killing emerged but was quickly swallowed in the unfolding drama. One of the survivors, Josephat Oldioi Ndooko, said the herdsmen were discussing the current drought outside the fence when security personnel arrived. The surviving herdsmen vowed not to withdraw their livestock from the ranch since there was no pasture in community lands and their livestock risked starving to death.[24] A few years previously, severe drought in Laikipia had led to pastoralists "invading" white-owned ranches. When the ranchers had tried to drive the pastoralist cattle away, then President Daniel arap Moi had intervened and urged some kind of accommodation between the two groups, a proposal to which the ranchers acquiesced. In the charged atmosphere created by the land restitution campaign, Ntinai ole Moiyare's death was merged with the drama of land invasion. The swift intervention of the State was a clear indication that the campaign was now being regarded as a fundamental assault on the sanctity of property rights in modern Kenya.

Events moved rapidly thereafter. The Rift Valley Provincial Commissioner – who had been "ambushed" with the Maasai petition a week before – placed the Provincial Security Committee on high alert. He immediately ordered the deployment of police helicopter units, additional police and GSU ground contingents. He also called in the highly experienced Anti-Stock Theft Unit. Police and the Anti-Stock Theft Unit were ordered to patrol ranches in Laikipia, Naivasha and Nanyuki. The district administration reiterated a warning from the Lands Minister that Maasai "invading ranches in Laikipia will only have themselves to blame [for the consequences]." Laikipia District Commissioner Wilson Njenga said the Segera Ranch youth would be charged with encroaching on private property. Seventy Maasai herdsmen within the vicinity of Loldaiga were arrested that same day.

The security operation shifted into another gear. On instructions from the ranchers, the press was denied entry to the ranches.[25] This was clearly no ordinary police job. It was, as the details trickling out would reveal, a punitive operation. An MCSF team touring Laikipia in the aftermath of the security operation interviewed residents who claimed the security personnel had raped an unspecified number of women and, in Rumuruti, castrated at least three men. Houses had been torched and household goods stolen and destroyed. The arrested herdsmen, now regarded as invaders, were held in various police stations within Laikipia district. They were not arraigned in court until the middle of September 2004, and were denied food, water and any contact with visitors. In addition, security personnel had confiscated cattle and other livestock, the equivalent of freezing bank accounts. And as if to add some bizarre festivity to the operation, smoke was seen rising from the police station compound the whole time during the operation. The smell of *nyama choma* (roast meat) filled the air.[26]

"They got their maths wrong"
In Nairobi, a second attempt at presenting the petition to the Lands Minister and the British High Commissioner on August 24th 2004 was foiled when police descended on a group of demonstrators and, in full view of TV crews, proceeded to severely beat up and arrest the demonstrators. Over 30 were charged with incitement in

the High Court in Nairobi a few hours later. That same evening, Lands Minister Amos Kimunya appeared at a televised press conference. He dismissed the Anglo-Maasai Agreements as invalid, saying that any historical obligations to the Maasai had been dispensed with at independence when a new nation was born. He also repudiated Maasai claims that the Laikipia leases had expired. The Maasai, he said, had got their maths wrong. The treaties were valid for 999 years, not 99 years, as the Maasai had claimed. Mining a vein of his own private wit, he continued: "They should come back in another 900 years and we can discuss the matter, although I suspect things will have changed a little." The State was clearly responding to Western fears generated by the foreign media accounts, not the expectations of its domestic constituency. It had acted precisely in order to reassure the West that its interests would be protected. And there was a sub-text here that recalled a covenant from another age: That of the nationalist elite's commitment to the protection of settler and/or foreign interests. Both the letter and spirit of Kenyatta's Nakuru Covenant were still alive.[27]

Back at the ranch, so to speak, a cloud of amnesia floated over the state security cordon. When the media was finally allowed access to Laikipia a week after the security alert had been placed, they found a ranching community gripped by sudden and debilitating memory loss. Ranchers interviewed could not remember how long their own land leases were supposed to last, were unaware of the Anglo-Maasai agreement, and, in at least one case, were unable to produce title deeds to their ranches. And when opinion *was* expressed, it bordered on the absurd: the "invaders", observed Ms. Odile de Weck, who had inherited her father's 3,600-acre Loldoto Farm, were not genuine – not Maasai at all. They were, she noted emphatically, Kikuyus. The Maasai, she said, had willingly ceded rights to Laikipia, had been compensated long ago and now resided happily in some other part of Kenya, far away.[28] A Mr. Jack Kenyon, who could not produce the annual lease payment receipts to his 16,000-acre ranch, *had* heard of the Anglo-Maasai "lease" agreement but was not sure of its contents. It was all very confusing. He urged government arbitration. Now that the government was actively nursing settler interests, it was safe to play dumb. However, in stating so unequivocally where its loyalties lay, the State knew that it had exposed a trait that many of its critics had begun to accuse it of possessing: elitist contempt for *wananchi* (ordinary citizens).[29]

In reacting so violently to the Maasai campaign, it had confirmed the accusations. It needed to minimise the damage. In order to do so effectively, the Maasai campaign had to be criminalised. Their claims had to be corrupted, divested of agency. The campaign, as was standard State practice, had to be portrayed as a conspiracy conceived by foreign-funded agitators.[30] Under cover of this conspiracy, vulnerable areas of the offending body would then be identified, isolated and exposed as contaminated. The public had to be convinced of the distinction between the State's *use* of violence and the enemy's agenda that carried the *potential* for violence. For this, the rule of law would be deployed: *they* are breaking the law; *we* are enforcing it. The tactics had been taken, word-for-word, play-for-play from the Moi-era single-party rule-book.

"There are some NGOs who are inciting the Maasai for their own gain," announced Lands Minister Kimunya, sounding like a member of the Moi regime at the height of single-party rule.[31] The State's counter-strategy followed the familiar Moi-era patterns of harassment and intimidation. So in Laikipia, "relatives of 44 Maasai herdsmen charged with invading white-owned ranches were left in shock after a Nyeri court ordered them to pay a total of 3.5 million shillings" (approximately 25,000 pounds sterling).[32] The charges would later be dropped without explanation. State authorities also seized computers, files and other material from the offices of the Laikipia-based NGO Osiligi, and froze its accounts. Osiligi was the NGO referred to as "inciting" the Maasai. Its fate at the hands of the State was calculated to serve as a warning to members of the wider campaign.

The Maasai had the tacit sympathy of the public and the steady spotlight of the media. They exploited the two ruthlessly. And in Sempeta and others, they had articulate defenders among themselves. In addition, veteran Maasai political leaders, both within the Cabinet and elsewhere, were shouting their distant support. Sempeta and other pro-Maasai lawyers were quite prepared to challenge the primacy of settler property rights by using the argument that the Anglo-Maasai treaties were illegal. While seeming to relent on the issue of the leases – there was no direct evidence in the Agreements to support the claim that the leases had expired, or that the lease-expiry was linked to the Agreements at all – Sempeta went directly to the heart of the issue. "The Minister's position could be correct that the leases have not expired, but to give those Agreements a lease of one day is to strangle the whole system of law. The agreements are illegal...the basis upon which they were created is a forgery." The Maasai, he said, were demanding ownership of all the lands that had been alienated from them in the 1904 and 1911 Agreements. And they were demanding them directly from the British. Why? "The British own and control all the resources of this country...Kenya's independence is a fallacy and there is documentation that can prove it." [33]

The Maasai campaign seemed to unlock a national closet of contested claims. During the last weeks of August, the skeletons came clattering out. In the southern Rift Valley, the Kipsigis[34] alleged that parts of Kericho district, home to multinational-owned tea plantations, had been excised from them during the colonial era and never returned. No compensation had been paid to them and they therefore intended to reclaim the area. In the Mount Elgon area in the far west of the country, the Sabaot claimed that their ancestral land had been taken by the government. They were now demanding it back. Then there were the old flare-ups from the Pokot in the Northern Rift, repeating the charge that the colonial government had illegally taken a district, Trans-Nzoia, from them. They had received no compensation and had been forcibly moved to arid land.

Elijah ole Sempeta was driving into his Ngong residence one Saturday night in March 2005 when he was attacked and shot. He was found dead in his car moments later.

Apart from some money in his wallet, nothing was stolen. The killers have not been found.

Had he been assassinated? Many Ngong residents and Maasai campaigners believe so. Ngong is one of the biggest towns in Maasailand. Highly cosmopolitan – it is located about half an hour's drive from Nairobi – Ngong had been rocked by a spate of violence in the months prior to Sempeta's death. The killing seemed to follow a pattern of violence in the area that some suspect is linked to the State's anti-Maasai campaign. Whatever the case, his killing robbed the Maasai of one of their most charismatic and outspoken defenders.

The Maasai campaign speaks of the State's failure to institute a new constitutional order. It was born of a realisation that the State – whether in its colonial or post-colonial phase – was not just unwilling to address the community's grievances, but had an active interest in perpetuating them. *Uhuru* (independence), as is so often pointed out, merely led to a change of guard. Sempeta alluded to this when he said in an interview that independence was a myth.[35]

The nationalist elites profited hugely from retaining the colonial order. The State became a vehicle for the accumulation of private property and land – especially Maasai land – and became a tool to support an ethnic patronage system. The Maasai, therefore, needed to be *querbogen,* their silence perpetuated by the reinforcement of the stereotypes of "strangeness" and "primitivity". Beneath the silence is almost a century of increasing poverty and underdevelopment.

When the British arrived in Kenya, they cynically described the Maasai as "probably the richest uncivilised race in the world"; by the time of their departure, the Maasai had become among the poorest. By "exoticising" the Maasai, or at least encouraging that process, the post-colonial elite were able to deflect attention from Maasai grievances.

Notes

[1] *Shuka* means blanket in Kiswahili, and is the term used for the cotton wrap-around that the Maasai have adopted as their traditional attire.

[2] Hughes, Lotte (2006), *Moving the Maasai: A Colonial Misadventure*, Basingstoke: Palgrave Macmillan. The Magadi Soda company was originally owned by Brunner, Mond & Co. When Mond was compulsorily wound up, the Magadi interest was taken over by ICI who sold it in the early 1990s to the Penrice Group, a Canadian company. It reverted to its Brunner, Mond before recently being acquired by the Tata Group of India.

[3] See Brunner, Mond & Co. official website: www.brunnermond.com

[4] Maa Civil Society Forum, "A Memorandum on the Anglo-Maasai Agreements: A Case of Historical and Contemporary Injustices and the Dispossession of Maasai Land", 13 August 2004.

[5] Ibid.

[6] The National Rainbow Coalition (NARC) came into power in December 2002 after ousting Daniel arap Moi, who had ruled the country since 1978.

[7] Brantley, Cynthia (1981), *The Giriama and Colonial Resistance in Kenya, 1800-1920*, Berkeley: University of California Press.

[8] "Maasai Demand 'Their' Land From British Ranchers" *East African Standard*, 14 August 2004.

[9] Ibid.

[10] *Daily Nation*, 14 August 2004.

[11] Dr. Krapf's revised and rearranged *Swahili-English Dictionary* (originally published in 1925 and re-published in 2006) gives the meaning of *mzungu* as: "a European; something wonderful, startling, surprising, ingenuity, cleverness." (Dr. J.L. Krapf was a missionary of the Church Missionary Society and commenced his work in East Africa in 1844.) *Mbenzi* is a Kiswahili-ism popularised by the Kenyan author Ngugi wa Thiong'o. It means literally, "he of the [Mercedes] Benz", and is used as a signifier for the African *nouveau riche* of the immediate post-independence generation. It is somewhat anachronistic today, but I can't think of a better word to describe the nationalist elite.

[12] "Establishing the Pax Lenana in Maasailand", *Daily Nation*, 22 July 22 2004, also 5 August 2004.

[13] The reference is to Sir Charles Eliot (1902), *East Africa Protectorate*, London.

[14] For the story of the 1990s clashes, see Oucho, John O.(2002),

Undercurrents of Ethnic Conflict in Kenya, Leiden, Boston & Koln: Brill.

[15]Hartley, Aidan (2004),"Cargo Cult", *The Spectator,* 28 August.

[16]"Maasai demand 'their' land back", *East African Standard,* 14 August 2004. The quote is attributed to Elijah ole Sempeta.

[17]"Masai Invaders Target Last White Farmers", *Daily Telegraph,* 13 August 2004.

[18]Marc Lacey, "Tribe, Claiming Whites' Land, Confronts Kenya Government", *New York Times,* 24 August 2004.

[19]"Masai Invaders Target Last White Farmers", *Daily Telegraph,* 13 August 2004.

[20]"Moran shot dead in farm invasion', *East African Standard,* 23 August 2004.

[21] Ibid.

[22] Ibid.

[23] Ibid.

[24] Ibid.

[25]Ibid.

[26]Statement by Joseph ole Simel, Manyoito Pastoralists Integrated Development Organisation (MPIDO), corroborated by interviews in August 2004.

[27]A few months after Kenya gained independence, first President Jomo Kenyatta addressed the white settler community in Nakuru, Rift Valley Province, who were very nervous about their future in Kenya. In a famous and oft-quoted speech, he assured the white settler community that in the new dispensation "We will forgive but never forget." This implied both that their interests would be protected, and that it was also safe to re-invest in independent Kenya. It is a promise that has been faithfully kept by successive regimes.

[28]"Ranchers ignorant of 999-year lease", *Sunday Standard,* 29 August 2004. A similar story ran on Kenya Television Network, the broadcasting arm of the Standard Group.

[29]A popular example of this line of criticism can be found in the *Sunday Nation* op-ed column by political scientist Mutahi Ngunyi.

[30]During the struggle for the return of multiparty rule, the Moi regime often accused the multiparty movement of "being used by foreigners".

[31]"Maasai incited by selfish people", *East African Standard,* 1 September 2004.

[32]"Herders ordered to pay Sh 3.5 million", *East African Standard,* 1 September 2004.

[33]"Land war between Maasai, British", *East African Standard*

4

UNSETTLED

Kalundi Serumaga

I n January 2008, somewhere deep inside a rural forest in Kenya, young men were preparing for war. In a city slum, a man had just beheaded another who was on his way to work as a loader in the city's industrial area. In the lakeside town of Kisumu, vandals were ripping off the windows and doors of shops left behind by families fleeing post-election violence that had rocked the country since the announcement of flawed election results a few days earlier.

One theme runs through these events: debilitating poverty.

Normalising the abnormal

Poverty is the worst form of violence. At its worst, it is a form of slow genocide. For example, take the fact that the vast majority of Native Americans "rubbed out" in what can only be described as a genocide, died (and still die) not from settler bullets, but from poor diets, disease, poor-on-poor crime, stress-related illnesses caused by predatory lending and so on. In short, they are killed by the condition of being poor. Similarly, if Kibera in Nairobi is indeed the world's biggest slum, then it is also one of the single biggest acts of violence against African people, carried out over the longest period of time.

Poverty-stricken girls are worst affected as poverty exposes them to all sorts of deprivations that lead to deadly temptations; they fall prey to these temptations not because they are weak, but because they have no other choice. They grow up angry and enervated. Adults raised in poverty often suffer a certain furtive sense of shame and anger that they can never quite shake off. Years of "no" and "not enough" force them to ingest a bitter diet of silent rage, frustrations, thwarted dreams, hurtful choices and humiliation as their parents age prematurely before their eyes, and their siblings learn to mask all feelings of disappointment. It is violence at the deepest psychological, spiritual and emotional levels, long before it becomes physical.

I know. I've been there. In Kenya.

The disputed 2007 general elections in Kenya and the subsequent orgy of gratuitous blood-letting have given rise to expressions of grief, shock and anger from the Kenyan intelligentsia in a way that leaves me truly mystified. Have they not been paying attention? If money and land meant for the poor can be stolen from them, then why not votes? If it became a four-decade normality for Kenyan children to grow up sharing and eating rotting oranges from garbage cans, why on earth should they not share more direct forms of violence with each other? Having grown up witnessing Kenya's normalising of the grotesquely abnormal, my only surprise was that these acts – from the rigging itself to the rape, pillage and murder – took so long to reach this particular nadir. Kenya was, and is, an atrocity a long time made and a catastrophe a long time coming.

"There are no stories in the riots, only the ghosts of stories," as some wise black British woman said of Brixton and Handsworth a long time ago.

I should declare an interest: even though I spent some critical formative years living both near the top and the bottom of Kenyan society, I am not Kenyan. I was a refugee from another atrocity called Uganda, and part of a very politically-engaged community that was actively fomenting armed rebellion back home. Since our fight was political, we came to Kenya with a heightened interest in politics generally and were fascinated by the way in which the Jomo Kenyatta and Daniel arap Moi regimes were "sowing acres of cynicism" (to quote Okot p'Bitek, another Ugandan refugee) in the country, something both Idi Amin and Milton Obote could only attempt through planting killing fields.

The current president, Mwai Kibaki, was a particularly

interesting case study for us. As a graduate of Makerere University, we would wonder if he participated in politics with Ugandan or with Kenyan sensibilities. For me, he answered the question most eloquently when, as a Seriously Big Government Man, he toured a high-security prison way back in the 1970s. There had been media talk of increasingly horrific conditions in the prisons, and his visit was supposed to be a fact-finding mission. At one point, as Big-Man-And-Entourage walked through the prison complex, a prisoner displayed incredible dignity and courage by stepping out in front of him and trying to hand him a letter sealed in an envelope. The prison official next to Honourable Kibaki intercepted the convict's outstretched hand, took the envelope and pocketed it. According to a news report, Kibaki paused, watched the entire incident, and then carried on with his fact-finding.

Forget about Kibaki's recent botched attempts to write a new constitution, forget about his failure to follow up on grand corruption, forget even about the indignity of getting himself sworn in as president at twilight, minutes after the disputed election results were announced. For me, looking back, it was at that moment that Kibaki disqualified himself from being president of anywhere or anything. It's just that nobody realised it, or thought about it hard enough. Now look where the country has ended up.

Tea without biscuits

Jeffrey had two thumbs on his left hand, but that was not the most interesting thing about him. He drove a little pick-up truck for one of the large tea estates in the Limuru area where I went to school, and would often give us a lift back up to our hillside campus after we had been hiking or running in the countryside.

Jeffrey lived in the tea plantation, but not in a house. His home was a large garage. He lived there with his wife, kids and mother. During the day, they would just slide the huge door open and leave it that way like some large gaping wound. As we walked or jogged past, you could see them all gathered inside, going about their domestic business as if on a cinema screen.

One day Jeffrey drove us much higher up the hill where one had a clear view of much of the valley below. He was really talking to my classmate Karim Walji, but I remain grateful to him for the education he gave us. Using large, lonely trees, hillocks and dips in the valley as landmarks, the three-thumbed Kikuyu man, living in a *mzungu* (white settler)'s garage on his own ancestors' land, listed for us the families and clans that had lived there before the endless carpet of green tea was violently laid down.

"Where did all the people go?" Karim asked. Jeffrey put on a wan smile. As somebody who had been smuggled across a border on the back of a pedal-bike to a new and more "stable" country, I felt strangely disturbed. But I understood that smile, and the inability to say more (our parents seemed stuck in that mode), but I was scared at how normal this dispossession had become. At least we were fighting those who had evicted us, not living in their garages. But now we were living in Kenya, where the abnormal was normal.

Don't hunt what you can't kill

"Don't go to town today, they are rounding up Ugandans." This was regularly-heard advice in the Ugandan exile community as Kenyans pointed us out to their police. A night or two cleaning their police cells or a well-deployed bribe was what was needed to keep you from joining a refugee camp or being left to rot in a prison. On reflection, it made sense for people oppressed by their own police force to be more than happy to point out other more vulnerable victims to the same police.

Wakimbizi (refugees) have no permanence, no power to come back later and retaliate. They are perfect victims, and probably help to deflect police attention from the native poor. Now, displaced and poor working Kenyans find themselves the new targets, but without the help of the police. If you kill a cop, ten will come back to kill you; if you kill a child of the rich, your fellow poor will be offered reward money to find you. And if you kill a fellow poor "non-you", you have found the perfect victim.

How else are the poor, schooled in forty years of

systemic violence, expected to communicate except through violence? Who do they vent their rage on except another guaranteed to have no power to retaliate with greater force?

Those who managed to escape poverty also internalised the violence. Having perfected the skills of managerial service provision, the Kenyan middle classes have moved to dominate top positions in the media, financial services, NGO and hospitality sectors throughout the East Africa region, where they have acquired the reputation of being the most cut-throat, ruthless, backstabbing, neurotic and efficient of Boardroom-wallahs.

Not yet uhuru

The crisis that is Kenya today is largely a result of the Kenyan intelligentsia's abject failure to come up with viable alternatives to this mess. Those in power never had the answers, and are not interested in looking for them. Like Uganda, the creation of Kenya was an act of theft and murder. Anyone managing it is simply perpetuating those crimes. Those in opposition had a responsibility to come up with something better. But did they?

With my two teenage brothers, I wandered the streets of Nairobi on August 1st, 1982, the day some members of Kenya's air force attempted a coup. As we walked from the low-income neighbourhoods of Eastleigh through Majengo then downtown, up to Hurlingham and back, we saw air force mutineers using their Land Rovers to wrench the metal grills from shop fronts and then say *"chukua"* (take) to the waiting looters. There was a lot of shouting of "Power", but no answers about poverty, certainly not for the half-naked man lying in the street at their feet, his whole body ashen grey from the blood loss occasioned by the open wound in his head. He was nobody's concern. He reminded me exactly of another half-naked dying man I had seen years before as a child in Kampala. He had been attacked by a mob. Or shot. Nobody was saying; just walking past. He was also lying in the gutter, also bleeding from the head, also barely twitching as he drew his very last breaths. Their ashen greys were a perfect match.

In the 1980s, a good Ugandan friend of mine found this whole tragedy perfectly summed up while on a necessary visit to a Nairobi public toilet. There was clearly no toilet paper, he narrated, so somebody before him had used his finger to clean his behind, and then wiped the shit on the toilet wall. On closer inspection (my friend is insatiably curious, no matter what the circumstances), he realised that this person had used the shit to write something on the toilet wall.

The word was *"uhuru"* – the Kiswahili word for freedom.

Part 2:
THE DEVELOPMENT SET

5

THE POWER OF LOVE

Binyavanga Wainaina

I was 14 years old when *We are the World* filled our television screens – and I discovered that we are loved. That was an amazing kind of love: a giant chorus of exotic-looking people coming together as one, and they pouted and gurgled and they agreed. Yeah, yeah. Once in a while one of them would bend forward as if they were retching their love for Ethiopia from a really deep place in their belly, a personal testimony, and I knew it was true the world would be a better place, for you-uu-uu, and for me-ii-ii.

And there was this guy, who looked pale and thin and bruised, with wispy brown English hair, like Jesus had, who suffered for us, abandoning Boomtown Rats and Stray Cats to reach out and touch. And he is now the king of Ethiopia.

Then Canada did the same in a weepy song called *Tears are not Enough*. Vowels wobbled, words stretched out. Tears, tears, are not Enou-ou-ou-gh.

And the French gurgled, L'Ethiopieeeeeeeeeeee....ohhh! L'Ethiopeeeeee.

In the years since then, much love has poured into my city, Nairobi. For The Girl Child, for many hundreds of Awarenesses, for Poverty Eradication, for the Angelina Jolification and Anti-Desertification of Semi-Arid Regions in Sahelian Countries.

The resources poured in have been incredible: tens of thousands of 4X4s are tearing the country apart looking for a project to love. It used to be that big expensive cars were needed by the Fathers of Our Nations, so they could Develop Our Nations. Now, the Lovers of Our Nations are here to Develop Our Nations, and of course, they need cars to be efficient. Standards must be maintained. Things need to be run to International Standards.

Rents in Nairobi are now at par with Europe, to service the tens of thousands of Kenya-loving people who run Kenya-loving projects to save Kenyans and the Sudanese and others from Misery. Restaurants with names like Casablanca and Java and Lord Errol feed these people at a very high standard, and many parts of Nairobi look like New York City. And we are very excited about this. We have a German school, a French school, a Swedish school and an International School. This means Nairobi is developing very fast. You can get a cappuccino in Loki – a giant refugee camp in Northern Kenya.

I have learned that I, we, are a dollar-a-day people (which is terrible, they say, because a cow in Japan is worth $9 a day). This means that a Japanese cow would be a middle-class Kenyan. Now, a dollar-a-day person cannot know what is good for him – which means that a $9-a-day cow from Japan could very well head a humanitarian NGO in Kenya. Massages are very cheap in Nairobi, so the cow would be comfortable.

Nairobi is crawling with $5-a-day, 25 year-old backpackers who came and loved and compassioned and are now the beneficiaries of $5,000 a month jobs consulting for the United Nations (CV: After working in bars in London, I was involved in a tobacco-harvesting project near the gorilla sanctuary in Uganda when the overland truck was stranded for five days, and I taught schoolchildren to sing *Born in the USA*), while Master's students from Kenya are selling fruit by the side of the road for a dollar a day, and live in Kibera slum, the only place where rent is cheap, but this may change since Ralph Fiennes went and loved Kibera. (Am I the only person who thought Fiennes's wife in the film *The Constant Gardener* was sleeping with the black doctor, only to discover that the black doctor was gay? The doctor was a placebo to political correctness, to authenticate the movie, just like an ineffectual Steve Biko authenticated *Cry Freedom*, showing how Donald Woods rescued South Africa from apartheid. The doctor cannot affect the narrative – the true saviours of his country are Fiennes and Rachel Weisz. But they love him. They really love the good gay doctor. They would never sleep with him on screen, though.)

Last year, I met a lovely young woman from England, all of 19, who came all the way to Naivasha, to a specific location very near a lovely lake, next to several beautiful game sanctuaries and a lodge run by her boyfriend's father. But these were not her concern. She was in Kenya to teach the people of some peri-urban location how to use a condom. She told me that she talks to groups of men and shows them how a condom can save their lives. I asked her whether there were no nurses or teachers who could do this at maybe a tenth or one hundred-thousandth of the cost it would take to keep her in this lovely and rather expensive location, and her eyes melted and she said, "But I care about people. Can't you see people are dying? Something must be done."

"In my gap year."

She did not add.

I was very moved.

Various royal princes have been here in their gap years, and we have seen them planting a tree or hugging a baby. One famous actress will adopt all the babies of Africa. And the Strategic Development Goal of that is that in 15 years, the Hollywood Bratpack will be Ethiopian and they will sing a song to save Ethiopia in a more authentic manner.

Many of our schoolchildren have been raised to Awareness, and this is thrilling news, that they are now aware. And every so often, on television, we are treated to schools' music festival poems by six-year olds, which go something like this:

The Girl Child! Let us all educate
The Girl Child!
The Girl Child!
For our Millennium Development Goals
The Girl Child! The Girl Child!

In 1995, I got a part-time job with a cotton ginnery in Mwea district that my father had invested in. My job was to meet with farmers in the dry areas and encourage them to grow cotton. It was not difficult to do – the farmers wanted to grow cotton, but lacked a market. Throughout those few months I heard talk of a legendary African king called PlanInternationo. People said that PlanInternationo gave them water and tanks and school fees, and every chief and government official I met went all moist talking about this king.

One day we went to the Thika district agricultural office to talk to the extension officers, whose *paid* job it is to advise farmers on their options. They asked us if we had been to see the people at PlanInternationo. We said no. They looked rather sad. We asked them if they could give us a person to take us around to meet farmers. They said yes, for some unaffordable number of dollars a day, many more than nine, or 90, they would. We can't afford that, I said. Oh, but that's what PlanInternationo pays, they said. They love us very much!

Then I met a senior guy at one of the big Humanitarian Agencies in Kenya, who said he wants to bring Bono to perform a concert in Mogadishu. To raise awareness.

Late in 2005 we heard that people were starving to death in many places all over Kenya. Immediately, the government urged the donor community to help. And the donor community urged the world community to help. And we saw large sad eyes of many nameless people on the very verge of death; and caring spokespeople, all white and tanned, told the world: People are dying!

Meanwhile our government had broken all tax collection records, and in other parts of Kenya, we were having huge bumper harvests. People died.

The most-loved people in Africa are the tall, thin noble people who were once or are still nomads and who live near Wild Animals. The Pokot, the Samburu, the Maasai have received more love than anybody in the world.

I met a woman at a dinner in New York who resembles and speaks like Scarlett O'Hara (My dadee this, my dadee that) who said she was a friend of Rafe (Fiennes). Scarlett is about to start producing handbags from the tails of Mongolian horses and she Just Luuurves Kenya and she is building a clinic for the Maasai people and sending a group to London to sing about manhood ceremonies to raise money. Nobody, really, has seen how the Maasai have become wealthy or even healthy out of all the thousands and thousands of Projects. But the Maasai, they can be certain that they are loved.

What you can be sure about in all these love projects is that it is easier for a thirty-something Scarlett O'Hara – or a Boomtown Rat – than it is for a PhD-wielding Maasai speaking, Maasai person, to decide who the Maasai will be to the world.

Because that is the Power of Love.

6

UN BLUES

Isisaeli Kazado

The realisation that he is white in a black country, and respected for it, is the turning-point in the expatriate's career. He can either forget it, or capitalise on it. Most choose the latter.

– Paul Theroux, "Tarzan is an Expatriate", *Transition 32*

The sprawling, lush 140-acre United Nations complex in Nairobi's upmarket Gigiri area serves as the headquarters of two global UN programmes and houses the regional and country offices of almost all of the UN's specialised agencies, funds, programmes and related agencies. Some 800 international staff and more than 2,000 national staff work within the Gigiri complex where fountains, fish ponds and crested cranes dot the landscaped gardens. A brochure proudly states that "Nairobi's UN Gigiri Complex stands as a potent symbol of the United Nations' commitment to equitable social and economic development, and to breaking the shackles of poverty on the world's poorest continent" [1].

The brochure further claims that the UN presence in Kenya contributes $350 million annually to the Kenyan economy and to the country's social development. An internal UN report released in 2000 found that about half of this contribution accrues from myriad spin-offs such as transport, international conferences and secondary employment of gardeners, guards, drivers, nannies and other house staff. Without any hint of irony, the *Financial Times* (which reported the findings of the report) stated: "House rents around the Gigiri area of Nairobi have soared, with popular UN residential areas fetching almost

$1,700 a month compared to around $750 for properties in other affluent suburbs."[2] What the *Financial Times* failed to report was that this enormous disparity in rents has created a two-tier society in Nairobi – one for the non-elite locals and other for the local elite and international expatriate crowd. The average rent paid in the city's slums, for instance, is $10 a month; in Umoja and other low-income estates, it is about $100 a month. Average per capita income in this relatively prosperous but highly unequal city is estimated to be less than $200 a month, the equivalent of what a mid-level UN international staff member earns in a day.

An unequal relationship

Because of the huge disparity between expatriate and local standards of living, UN and other development workers in Nairobi are easily distinguishable: they are normally seen driving around in huge SUVs with diplomatic licence plates and tend to hang around Gigiri and its environs, rarely venturing into the city centre for fear of being mugged, or worse, carjacked; UN staff members are routinely sent weekly advisories about which areas to avoid, how to evade carjackers and which security equipment to install in their heavily fortified mansions.

Working in a country where one's standard of living is substantially higher than that of the non-elite locals can, however, generate enormous feelings of guilt. Maria Eriksson Baaz, a Swedish researcher who spent some time studying the lifestyles and attitudes of European development workers in Tanzania, one of the poorest countries in the world, describes the feelings of "estrangement" that expatriates feel while working in a country where their daily incomes amount to the annual incomes of local peasants. Writes Baaz:

> Such feelings, which articulate the contradiction between the discourse of solidarity and the unequal living conditions, can of course be handled in different ways. One option is to avoid being exposed to, and reminded of, the inequalities. One way to minimise one's exposure is to socialise with people who

have a similar lifestyle – which generally means other expatriates. In this way, alienation and guilt seem to shape the formation of wazungu (white) communities.[3]

In cities such Dar es Salaam and Nairobi, UN employees spend their leisure time eating out, throwing dinner parties, visiting game parks or shopping. Being away from their extended families back home also means they have fewer responsibilities towards pesky and needy parents or siblings. This means they have more time to devote to their work. Baaz explains:

Development workers have the option, should they so wish, of devoting all their time and energy to their work. As a consequence of their standard of living and their being fully insured, they do not have to devote time or energy to the task of finding money to pay for food, health care, and so on. This does not mean, however, that development workers have no concern with issues related to material living conditions; considerable amounts of time and energy are indeed devoted to discussing issues such as car and child-benefit policies, solar panels, hot water, computers and so forth. The important point, though, is that, in contrast to the expatriate development workers, their Tanzanian colleagues are preoccupied with the question of survival. Due to low salaries, most have to engage in other income-generating activities outside formal work in order to make ends meet.[4]

Which is not to say that there are no economic or social hierarchies within the expatriate development community itself. As Baaz explains, there is a clear demarcation between "hard core" development workers who have a close, direct relationship with local communities, such as doctors working for Médecins Sans Frontières (MSF) or young, bright-eyed British volunteers working for Voluntary Services Overseas (VSO)[5] and their better-paid and pampered colleagues in organisations such as the United Nations who are perceived as people who "spend their lives at the Sheraton cocktail bar or the yacht club"[6] instead of doing serious development work.

Capacity-building, empowerment and other myths

In many war-torn nations and so-called developing countries, the UN enters on the promise of "strengthening the capacity of governments" and "empowering local communities". What this usually means is providing highly paid technical "experts" (some barely out of university) to oversee a UN-managed project in a poor country by holding expensive poverty reduction seminars in five-star hotels, or conducting training workshops for government officials on how to manage their affairs. (With "good governance" gaining more currency in UN circles, the latter have become more frequent.)

Much of the funding for the project ends up not with the poor, but with well-paid UN staff and consultants. In a discussion with Hastings Chikoko of the World Conservation Union, Rwanda's President Paul Kagame could not have put it more succinctly:

> There are projects here worth only $5 million, and when I looked at their expenses, I found that $1 million was going into buying cars, each of them at $70,000. Another $1 million goes to buying office furniture, more than $1 million for meetings and entertainment, yet another $1 million as salaries for technical experts, leaving only $1 million for the actual expenditure on a poverty reducing activity. [7]

Shortly after that interview in 2005, Kagame's Cabinet decided to impound all luxury four-wheel-drive cars belonging to the government, and to ban the holding of all workshops, seminars and conferences on poverty reduction in posh hotels, such as the Mille Collines and the InterContinental in Kigali.

The problem lies in the fact that, on the one hand, the "development set" advocates poverty reduction and development; on the other, it is this chaotic and impoverished world that provides it with its *raison d'etre* and gives it legitimacy. Like hyenas that watch from afar as lions eat their kill, and then help themselves to the leftovers, development workers have the unenviable task of waiting on the sidelines and going in only after the war is over, when the refugees have already crossed the border, when the drought has turned into a famine or when slums have become permanent cesspools of misery.

Even for the little money that ends up with the beneficiaries (now called "development partners"), there is little to show for it. As Clare Short, Britain's former International Development Secretary, has admitted, aid has failed to either reduce poverty or improve the lives of people in the poorest countries. (Ironically, Ms. Short was responsible for disbursing much of this aid.) Questioning the value of aid during a heated debate within the British parliament in 2003, she noted that Tanzania, one of the most aid-dependant countries in Africa, had remained poor despite a massive influx of donor funds.[8] "Tanzania has 1,000 major projects running at any one time, each with its own bank account and foreign monitors. That means around 2,000 aid missions a year, a recipe for making already weak ministries weaker still," she added.[9]

The problem with donor-funded programmes is that instead of making governments more accountable to their own citizens, government ministries end up spending much of their time meeting the demands and requirement of donors. Ashraf Ghani, Afghanistan's Minister of Finance from 2002 to 2004, lamented the strain of keeping up with donor demands, which include providing periodic audits of how donor money is spent:

> As Finance Minister, more than 60 per cent of my time was spent on managing donors, in terms of meeting visiting missions and representatives to reiterate government policy, raise funds...to enable the recurrent costs of government to be met, advocate for support to government-led programmes channelled through government financing, procurement, and accounting systems, and discuss and negotiate projects...This time could instead have been devoted to raising domestic revenue and managing internal reform.[10]

"Missions" (UN jargon for business class travel to exotic locations to attend conferences and hold meetings with government officials to advise them on how to run their countries, plan projects and strategise on poverty reduction programmes, interspersed with expensive dinners, shopping expeditions and the odd safari or sight-seeing tour), inevitably lead to the production of lengthy and obtuse documents and reports, most of which are never read. Although many UN reports, such as the UNDP's *Human Development Report*, are invaluable research tools, many others, such as those emanating from UN governing bodies, poverty reduction conferences and workshops, fact-finding or technical advisory missions and the like are read only by bored development workers or those charged with writing and editing them.

Many of these "missions" would not be necessary if UN and humanitarian agencies weren't competing with each other to service the poor, the homeless and the diseased. For instance, shortly after the Indian Ocean tsunami destroyed several settlements and killed thousands of people on Boxing Day 2004, every UN agency – regardless of its mandate – vied to be part of the humanitarian effort in the countries most affected. The race to be the first on the ground was so stiff that the United Nations Office for the Coordination of Humanitarian Affairs (OCHA) was forced to mediate these efforts to avoid duplication and to ensure that funds raised went to organisations with the most experience in post-disaster rehabilitation and reconstruction.

The realisation that many UN agencies end up duplicating – and sometimes negating – each others' work led a high-level UN panel to convene a meeting in November 2006 to propose radical reforms aimed at streamlining the organisation. The executive director of the panel noted that in some African countries, there were HIV/Aids advisors from five different UN agencies and that since the 1992 Earth Summit in Rio de Janeiro, over 30 UN agencies, funds and programmes had devoted nearly 400 meeting days a year to biodiversity, climate change, desertification and related subjects.[11] (Ironically, these meetings and conferences translate into more air travel, itself a contributor to global warming and climate change. According to the Intergovernmental Panel on

Climate Change, the world's airliners are responsible for 3.5 per cent of man-made global warming. Other surveys show that each airline passenger travelling from say, New York to Nairobi, produces over a tonne of carbon dioxide, the very quantity that each human being will be entitled to emit in a year if climate change policies are implemented.)

More meetings and conferences also mean more reports. In 2002, in an attempt to reform how the United Nations does business, UN Secretary-General Kofi Annan issued a report that revealed the following startling findings about the reports produced by the UN Secretariat in New York:

In 2000-2001, a staggering 15,484 meetings were held and 5,879 reports were issued...Reports are overwhelming in number, tend towards duplication and are fragmented in their impact. Member states, especially small countries, find it difficult to cope with the mountains of paper that need to be absorbed and acted upon. The Secretariat itself is struggling to keep abreast of the growing number of reports requested by the various intergovernmental bodies. The sheer volume of the demands is drowning its ability to provide focused and value-added analysis. [12]

One report Annan should have read – and acted upon –- was the one sent to him by the head of the UN's peacekeeping mission in Rwanda, General Romeo Dallaire, who in a faxed message to Annan's military advisor, warned of an impending genocide in Rwanda four months before the killings began. Annan, who was head of the UN's Department of Peacekeeping Operations at the time, rejected Dallaire's request to seize an arm cache and to evacuate an informant called Jean-Pierre, as such actions "went beyond the mission's mandate".[13] In his book *Shake Hands with the Devil*, Dallaire talks of being extremely "frustrated" with his inability to convince the UN Secretariat in New York to allow him to take actions that might have saved a few lives, if not prevented the genocide from occurring in the first place. "My failure to persuade New York to act on Jean-Pierre's information still haunts me," he wrote years later, in between the bouts of depression that he suffers from periodically as a result of what he views as his personal failure in Rwanda.[14]

It would be unfair to place all of the blame on the UN or its leaders, who after all, are not in a position to make any decisions without the approval of the Big Five governments – Britain, China, France, Russia and the United States – that control the UN Security Council. Their inaction on Rwanda is largely to blame. But even a moral stand on the issue would have been welcomed by not just the UN member states, but by African countries, not least Rwanda, which has consistently blamed the UN for the escalation of the conflict during those horrible 100 days in 1994.

Which is not to say that the UN has not contributed to peace and development efforts. This world body, through its various agencies, has contributed to eradicating smallpox from the planet, improving literacy, sheltering refugees, brokering peace agreements, alleviating hunger and promoting human rights in various parts of the world.

Unfortunately, most UN employees are more concerned about safeguarding their own salaries and benefits than safeguarding the rights of the world's people. This has led to a culture of sycophancy, mediocrity, inefficiency and corruption in various UN departments and agencies, behaviours that UN employees themselves admit are not tackled effectively. In a 2002/3 survey, for example, UN staff members generally felt that breaches of integrity and ethical conduct were not handled appropriately by the UN's disciplinary system and voiced concern about the consequences of "whistle-blowing".[15]

Sex, lies and red tape

As a consequence of the inherent inequality between "developers" and "developees", the relationship between expatriates and locals gets distorted in poor African countries because the point of contact between the two is essentially utilitarian; the latter either work for the former (as chauffeurs, nannies and the like) or are seen purely as "beneficiaries" of development assistance. This unequal relationship can, and does, lead to exploitative practices, including sexual abuse, especially in war-torn countries.

The Shame of War, a report published by OCHA in 2007 noted with alarm that sexual abuse of local women by UN peacekeepers and aid workers was becoming rampant in war-torn countries and explained why:

In situations where the vulnerable local population has been abused and is beleaguered by conflict, and where grinding poverty pervades, UN staff offer locals an increased degree of security as well as a much-needed influx of cash for goods and services. The dangerous combination of thousands of relatively well-paid young men posted overseas in environments where the rule of law and other societal constraints are often absent...has allowed the sexual abuse and/or exploitation of local populations. In some cases, the abuse has become more widespread as the behaviour continued unchecked...It is because international peacekeepers and aid workers have such an important physical and emblematic status – representing the international aspirations of human dignity, security and civilian protection – that their abuse of their position is considered, by many, so unacceptable...Peacekeepers and other international staff who engage in transactional sex in these environments – however willing the local women may appear – are de facto exploiting the very people they are supposed to protect.[16]

In some cases, the presence of UN peacekeepers can actually make security more precarious. Scandals involving the illegal sale of arms, especially in countries where militia control mineral-rich mines, by UN peacekeepers have also been reported. In May 2007, for instance, the BBC's Martin Plaut reported that in 2005, UN peacekeeping troops from Pakistan had been re-arming Congolese militia (who they were supposed to be disarming) in exchange for gold. A Congolese witness claimed to have seen a UN peacekeeper disarm members of the militia one day only to re-arm them the following day. The trade was allegedly being facilitated by a triad involving the UN peacekeepers, the Congolese army and traders from neighbouring Kenya. [17]

Incidents of abuse within the UN itself are often swept under the carpet, often on the pretext that the reporting of such incidents violates the UN code of conduct for staff members, which states that "loyalty to the aims, principles and purposes of the United Nations, as set forth in its Charter, is a fundamental obligation of staff members by virtue of their status as international civil servants".[18.] Nonetheless, in 2002, the UN's Ombudsman in Nairobi sent an internal memorandum to senior managers and the UN's staff union, which cited various allegations of abuse within the UN's Nairobi headquarters, including sexual harassment, discrimination, intimidation, bullying, abuse of authority and maladministration. The memo stated:

> The Ombudsman in Nairobi has lost count of the number of times petitioners have approached him seeking remedy for their colleagues, not for themselves, because the victims of abuse were too frightened to take action themselves...When asked why the victims themselves do not approach those supposedly in a position to help, they say their colleagues fear loss of contract, unfair dismissal, damage to career pathways, accusations of 'disloyalty', or other forms of retaliation or retribution. [19]

He further noted:

> The rights of the accused are so enshrined in the United Nations system of judicial fair play that there must be an overwhelming burden of proof for any accusation to be upheld. As a consequence, because most victims of abuse do not share their experiences (officially at least) with others, it is exceedingly difficult for them to demonstrate they have a solid case.[20]

The memo generated some panic within the corridors of the UN in Nairobi, but like all such memos, was quickly filed and forgotten. Predictably, when the Ombudsman, a jovial Icelander named Mik Magnusson, retired not long after the memo was circulated, his post was never filled. In fact, unconfirmed reports suggest that the post of

Ombudsman at the UN's Nairobi headquarters had been permanently scrapped.

Insiders say that this is because whistle blowing at the United Nations and its sister organisations, such as the World Bank, is neither encouraged nor tolerated. Anthony Van Vugt, a former World Bank employee, told *The Wall Street Journal* that the culture of conformity, silence and fear was so pervasive at the Bank that "as soon as you are seen blowing the whistle, your own colleagues won't even sit next to you in the cafeteria". [21]

Similarly, in a letter to the *Financial Times* of London, Professor Lawrence G. Franko, a veteran consultant to the World Bank and the United Nations, was even more scathing in his attack on multilateral bureaucracies.

> Back in my days...everyone knew that one of the major objectives of the multilateral bureaucracies was to provide highly renumerative employment and eternal job security for the boyfriends, girlfriends, pals, protégés, allies, not-too-noxious rivals, relatives and hangers-on of the political classes of all nations. The [World Bank] was an especially good resting place for would-be academics who could not obtain tenure at a competitive academic institution...This system was extraordinary at reducing poverty among the club of the world's development-intellectual mandarins. Whether it reduced poverty for actual poor people is highly debateable, and is becoming more so, especially in a world in which deep and flexible private capital markets, combined with increasingly responsible emerging market governments, are obviating the need for a single, huge 'World' Bank bureaucracy.[22]

"Healthy hotel bookings"

The irony is that despite all the evidence pointing to the failures of UN and other development agencies, and the misdemeanours perpetrated by the development set, Third World countries are the first to defend the presence of the United Nations and development workers in their countries. For instance, in February 2007, the Kenya government caused near panic in the country when then Environment

Minister Kivutha Kibwana reported a "plot" by rich countries to relocate the United Nations Environment Programme (UNEP) headquarters in Nairobi to Europe. One would have thought that the government's main concern would have been how this relocation might affect the country's privileged status as the host of a UN headquarters, but Andrew Kiptoon, Kenya's ambassador to UNEP, was more concerned about the UN employees' contribution to the national treasury (not through development assistance but by virtue of the fact that UN employees living in the country spend substantial proportions of their hefty salaries on local products and services). Noting that the UN was the third largest contributor to Kenya's economy after tourism and horticulture, he urged the UN staff to remain in the country and to continue holding international conferences in the capital city "because such conferences lead to healthy hotel bookings".[23]

Kenyan newspapers carried various opinions on the impact of the impending move; most of them claimed that upmarket shopping malls and supermarkets, real estate, recreation facilities and the local procurement chain in Nairobi would be hardest hit by the pullout. Others were less alarmist. An editorial in the *Sunday Nation* stated that the UN's relocation "would hurt the economy and the prestige of the city, but it would hardly bring the country to its knees."[24]

When UNEP announced that it had no plans to relocate, government officials and domestic workers employed by UN staff – maids, gardeners, cooks and drivers – were relieved; even more relieved were the owners of real estate agencies, shops and restaurants in the Gigiri area, who rely almost exclusively on their UN clientele for business.

Shop owners in the Village Market, a slick shopping mall a stone's throw away from the UN Gigiri complex, were most pleased. A hair stylist, who claimed that she charged "Europeans, ambassadors and their families" substantially higher rates for a hair cut than those she charged "locals and Africans", admitted to the *Daily Nation* that her interest in the UN presence in Nairobi was purely selfish and based on commercial interests. She claimed that the conspiracy to remove the UN from Kenya was "inhuman" because it would "deprive people like her of their livelihoods".

And using a logic that is both twisted and totally rational, a businesswoman explained that since UN employees bring so much business to people like her, they were helping to improve the economy and to reduce poverty in the country. Instead of calling for the relocation of the UN, she added, "The world should establish more international organisations in our country so we can develop".[25]

Notes

1 *United Nations Office at Nairobi: The UN Headquarters in Africa,* published in 2004/5.
2 Turner, Mark (2000), "UN Presence Keeps Kenyan Economy Afloat", *Financial Times* (London), 15 January.
3 Baaz, Maria Eriksson (2005), *The Paternalism of Partnership*, London and New York: Zed Books Ltd. p. 87
4 Ibid. p 92
5 Interview of a VSO officer in Baaz (2006), p. 83
6 Baaz (2006). p. 82
7 Chikoko, L. Hastings, "Why donors fear Kagame's war on graft", Posted on the World Conservation Union (IUCM) www.iucn.org
8 Tanzania, Ethiopia, the Democratic Republic of the Congo and Mozambique were the biggest recipients of development aid in 2003, according to UNDP's *Human Development Report 2005*, New York, table 19
9 Redfern, Paul (2003), "UK Debates Future of Aid to Third World Countries", *The East African,* February 10-17.
10 Quoted in: UNDP (2005) *Human Development Report 2005*, New York.
11 Leopold, Evelyn (2006), "Panel wants major overhaul of UN projects for the poor", *Reuters News*, 9 November.
12 Available at www.un.org/reform/
13 Pugliese, David (2002), "Dallaire's Mission: Part I: The Untold Story of the UN's disastrous peacekeeping mission in Rwanda and the Canadian soldier who must live with the consequences", *Ottawa Citizen*, 22 September.
14 Dallaire, Romeo (2003), *Shake Hands with the Devil*, Random House Canada.
15 The results of this survey were announced to UN staff by UN Secretary-General Kofi Annan on 4 June 2004.
16 OCHA/IRIN (2007), "Sexual abuse and exploitation by peacekeepers and aid workers", *The Shame of War,* Nairobi.
17 Plaut, Martin (2007), "UN Troops 'Traded Gold for Guns'," *BBC News*, 23 May.
18 UN Staff Rule 1.2e
19 "A situational analysis of abuse", internal memo issued by the office of the Ombudsman at the UN Office in Nairobi, 2002.
20 Ibid.
21 Stephens, Brett (2007), "The Whistleblower's Tale", *The Wall Street Journal*, 8 May. In 1995, Van Vugt had filed an ethics investigation

when he discovered that his managers had misappropriated $100,000 from a trust fund established to finance a project in the Philippines, an action which, ironically, led him to his being blacklisted from the organisation.

[22] Letter to the Editor, *Financial Times*, 9 May 2007.

[23] Mbaria, John (2007), "The Sh25.2 billion plot against Kenya", *Sunday Nation*, 11 February.

[24] *Sunday Nation* (2007), "We must fight off European plot against UNEP", 11 February.

[25] Mburu, Stephen (2007), "Shopping complex in city risks closure", *Daily Nation*, 11 February

7

A CHARITABLE APARTHEID

Lara Pawson

There is a fact: White men consider themselves superior to black men. There is another fact: Black men want to prove to white men, at all costs, the richness of their thought, the equal value of their intellect. How do we extricate ourselves?

– **Frantz Fanon,** *Black Skin, White Masks (1952)*

A treasure hunt was held in a West African capital city in the summer of 2004. It was a small affair. A young, female aid worker from North America was celebrating her birthday. Barbara (not her real name) invited a group of friends to take part in the hunt, which was followed in the evening by a party, involving lots of dancing and drinking. The treasure hunt had a slight twist; it wasn't strictly a hunt for treasure. Barbara thought it would be more fun to hold a photograph hunt, so, instead of clue-solving, the participants would take snaps of particular subjects. The list of pictures Barbara proposed included: a photograph of a local person urinating in public, a local man drinking beer, a local woman sitting on the back of a moped with something really large balancing on her head, and a local man watching a woman working.

The treasure hunt was held on a Saturday at the height of the hot season. Daytime temperatures were reaching 100 degrees Fahrenheit, sometimes higher. To avoid the heat, teams carried out the hunt in air-conditioned cars. Barbara nevertheless insisted that speed was not important because the competition would be judged on the quality and originality of each shot. The larger the object on top of the woman's head, for instance, the better the shot. Barbara's friends responded to the challenge with varying degrees of ingenuity.

One team decided to pay their African subjects cash to induce them to perform for the camera. This carload included a very senior US diplomat and an American Peace Corps volunteer turned businesswoman. From the comfort of their large car – possibly a D-plated vehicle – the team persuaded various people to pose. A young boy willingly peed at the side of the road and a man agreed to be photographed drinking a bottle of beer. Neither shot, however, was taken without problems. In the case of the urinating child, angry onlookers shouted at the group of expatriates to stop photographing the child. But the team still managed to get the shot they needed, pay the child and speed off, ignoring the complaints. Undeterred, they tracked down a roadside boutique where a woman was selling bottled beer. They called to a young man nearby and explained that they would pay cash if he would let them take a picture of him drinking a beer. He agreed. He went over to the boutique, took a bottle, plucked off the lid and began to drink. Once the bottle was dry, he asked his audience for the agreed payment. The hunters handed over the money, giving the young man enough cash to pay the boutique-owner for the beer as well. But their willing subject proved wilier than they had bargained for: he scarpered with all the money, leaving the woman out of pocket.

At this point, a row broke out between the treasure hunt team and the woman from the boutique. She insisted that they pay her for the bottle of beer. After all, it wasn't her fault that the man had stolen it. But the team refused to pay up, also claiming it was not their fault that the young beer drinker had run off with all the cash. The volume of their dispute increased and within minutes a crowd had gathered to observe the confusion. The woman from the boutique became increasingly distressed and started shouting for the police. Before long, the cops appeared. The row continued but eventually the foreigners were persuaded to pay the woman for her beer, which cost about 50 pence. The crowds melted and the hunters drove off.

Meanwhile, across town, another team had devised a more relaxing way to get their photographs: they would persuade a single African to enact each scenario. The easiest way to do this was to use a security guard from the home of a young North American man, one of the team members. Thus it was that a local man, employed by a foreign aid agency as a security guard, found himself performing for photographs that his youthful white boss needed for a bit of birthday fun.

Later, at the party, there was great hilarity as various participants in the treasure hunt recounted the events of the day. The party was held at the house of the senior US diplomat who had been involved in the beer contretemps earlier that day. This was in a wealthy suburb close to the banks of a wide river. It came with a large garden, a swimming pool and a terrace the size of a dance floor. A drinks trolley, loaded with every spirit or liqueur, wine or beer you might wish, was parked like a pram in the garden. There was a lot of discussion about whether or not the team that had used the guard should be disqualified for cheating. It was all very amusing.

Many of the treasure hunters were aid workers; others were diplomats or officials representing foreign donors. Barbara was a senior member of staff at a leading North American non-governmental organisation that promotes condoms for safe sex, particularly among "low-income and other vulnerable people'". Her young friend (a recent graduate), the one who deployed his security guard as a model, was running another NGO, which uses sport to teach "the world's most disadvantaged children... optimism, respect, compassion, courage, leadership, inspiration and joy". This was his first job in Africa and he was considered capable enough to lead an entire organisation in a foreign country. Other treasure hunters included staff working for the US government's aid department, the United States Agency for International Development (USAID). USAID prides itself on "a long history of extending a helping hand to those people overseas struggling to make a better life, recover from a disaster or striving to live in a free and democratic country". It is, claims USAID, "this caring that stands as a hallmark of the United States around the world".[1]

There is nothing straightforward, however, about this apparent benevolence. According to the USAID website, "US foreign assistance has always had the twofold purpose of furthering America's foreign policy interests in expanding democracy and free markets while improving the lives of the citizens of the developing world." In 2002, US aid to Africa totalled $3.2 billion (around 0.13 per cent of the total federal budget). The vast majority of aid is subject to strict conditions, most of which serve to promote the donor's interest: as much as 80 per cent of USAID's grants and contracts go directly to US companies and NGOs.[2] American aid is used, among other things, to promote the use of genetically modified crops. In the poor cotton-producing countries of West Africa, Monsanto, Syngenta and Dow AgroSciences, supported by USAID, are pushing GM cotton varieties into use, a move that is being resisted by local farmers. Like other donors, the Americans are masters at using aid as a stick to try to force recipient countries to support controversial aspects of foreign policy. For example, in 2003, the US suspended military aid to South Africa following a decision by the South African government not to grant Americans immunity from prosecution by the International Criminal Court in The Hague. There is little doubt that Africa would be better off if it sacrificed foreign aid (and subsequent debt) for fairer terms of trade with the rest of the world.[3] This is not simply an economic question, it is also a cultural-psychological one. Aid keeps Africa in a never-ending cycle of victimisation, forever subservient to the rich countries and their handouts.

The aid worker is the friendly face of this imperial foreign policy; charitable and humanitarian NGOs are the mechanism through which it is carried out. Many of these NGOs certainly provide useful and sometimes essential services. Their political impact, however, is compatible with several of the causes of the very problems they are meant to confront. As Arundhati Roy notes, NGOs often act as the frontline promoters of the neoliberal project, "accountable to their funders, not to the people they work among... It's almost as though the greater the devastation caused by neoliberalism, the greater the outbreak of NGOs." Worse still, they turn the receivers of aid into "dependent victims and blunt the edges of political resistance".[4] In some cases, foreign aid agencies act as a surrogate state, replacing and thus fragmenting the work of a nation's own government. When aid agencies like the UN's World Food Programme move in, African administrations tend to be let off the hook. But who can object? They're only there to help. The aid worker goes to Africa to care for the African, to make the African healthier and more democratic. Perhaps this explains why many expatriates – even a large number of those who are in Africa to "do good"'– so often resort to behaviour and attitudes that reveal a superiority complex reminiscent of colonialism.

Pride and prejudice
It is very rare in Africa to see white people treating Africans as equals, even in apparently trivial ways. These people are not the sort who join the British National Party. It's unlikely that they would even call themselves conservatives, let alone vote Tory or Republican. They are not the people in Europe or the United States who support a tightening of immigration laws or who remove their kids from a school that has "too many black kids". These are the very people who – according to their profession – want to help the developing world, who want to reduce poverty and believe, at least in principle, in equality. So, what is it that turns these apparently thoughtful and humane people into buffoons who find it easy to humiliate Africans and treat them as inferior beings? And what is it that allows African people to accept this?

From the moment a Western aid worker arrives in Africa, he or she joins the upper echelons of the social and economic hierarchy. His or her living standards are on a par with the local elite – a far cry from the average African household. For example, aid workers have their own transport: usually a large, white four-wheel drive. Many aid agencies seem to renew their vehicles with unnecessary frequency, so their four-by-fours are always shiny and clean. There is usually a local who is hired to clean the cars. That the vehicles are four-by-fours is not irrelevant: they are very large, powerful cars that guzzle fuel and cost a lot to keep on the road. Their size allows passengers a good view of the road and surrounding areas. If you have ever stood next to someone sitting in a four-wheel drive, you will also be aware that you have to look up at them; unlike a car, when you have to look down. So the large Land Rover, Cherokee, Landcruiser, Pajero or whatever it may be, gives the passenger an advantage of power – literally and metaphorically. Given that most Africans walk or take public transport, they are forever looking up at the fortunate foreigner, sealed into his large, air-conditioned, people-carrying unit. Another benefit of the four-by-four is that you can avoid the stare of the beggar far more easily than you would if you were walking, on public transport or in a smaller car that is lower to the ground. Foreigners can hide behind the thick glass quite easily, and may not have to confront their consciences as much as they would were they closer to the ground, closer to the outstretched hand of the beggar. Expatriates tend to be driven by a local driver: an aid worker is ferried about town by an African, often the same person who is in charge of cleaning the car.

There is an image in the West that Africa is the one place where four-by-fours are actually necessary. African roads are notoriously bad. And it is true that there are some areas to which you cannot travel if you don't have a four-wheel drive. However, it is amazing how many aid workers, UN staff, diplomats and some, though fewer, well-paid journalists, drive around urban areas in these enormous vehicles. You don't need a four-wheel drive in Bamako, for example, or in Ghana's capital, Accra. Even in the run-down Angolan capital Luanda, a city spilling over with people due to the recently ended civil war, a car is quite adequate. Plenty of people do well in a second- or third- or even fourth-hand saloon car. But in capital cities and towns throughout Africa, you can be sure of seeing a myriad shiny, often white, Landcruisers and Land Rovers buzzing about from staff residential areas to offices and back again. Why? Safety is one argument I have heard bandied about. But you are more likely to attract attention in a large car than if you drive about in a vehicle nobody would wish to steal. Apart from Johannesburg or Nairobi – where carjacking is a real threat to your daily safety – most African cities are safer than London. There's something else, too: many NGOs are strictly prohibited from providing lifts to locals.

However, let's move on – to housing. Most expatriates in Africa tend to live in the best houses available. Compounds are fairly common. They range from a few houses arranged around a cul-de-sac to 30 or 40 houses sandwiched between several streets. Whatever the size, the compound is characterised by high walls or fencing (sometimes electric) and guards (sometimes armed). Residents tend to be all-expatriate peppered with members of the local elite. Compounds offer security, convenience and exclusivity. At the top end of the scale, residents often have access to a shared swimming pool, tennis courts, ample parking space and other facilities. Not everyone lives in a compound. They may choose, instead, to live in separate accommodation, individual houses or apartments, usually found in the wealthy neighbourhoods or "blocks". It's not a coincidence that during the recent unrest in the Ivory Coast, much of the anger of President Laurent Gbagbo's young supporters was aimed at the exclusive neighbourhoods of the foreign elite.

Of course, there are exceptions. Some aid agencies – Médecins Sans Frontières, (MSF) springs to mind – put their foreign staff into one house and sometimes individuals share a room. Their facilities may include a generator plus a pretty yard – but hardly what, in Britain, would be described as luxury. Nevertheless, it is precisely on this point that the complexity of the foreigner's life in Africa begins. Most aid workers, UN staff, diplomats and reporters who go to work in Africa are viewed back home as plucky, hardy types who are roughing it under African skies to help carry the dark continent towards the light. However, from the vantage point of the locals, it is a different story. Expatriates – be they MSF "volunteers" or otherwise – enjoy a lifestyle that is beyond the wildest dreams of most Africans.

This sense of superiority has some very strange effects on people. Not so long ago, in Ivory Coast's commercial capital, Abidjan, I was derided by my colleagues for allowing a Ghanaian housemaid to stay inside the house. I was the acting West Africa correspondent for the BBC at the time and therefore was living in the BBC residence, a spacious bungalow with three bedrooms (each with en suite shower/bath facilities), a large dining room and, yes, a swimming pool. At the back of the bungalow was a narrow outhouse, which included a small bedroom for the maid. Unlike the bungalow, the maid's room lacked air-conditioning. However, during my three-month stay in Abidjan, I was only using two of the bedrooms in the main house. It seemed obvious to offer the spare room to the maid.

"You let her into the house?" That was the reaction I received from a young North American woman who was also staying in the BBC house with her partner. They were guests who had nowhere to live at the time because they were looking for their own luxury bungalow. But they were not at all happy about the arrangement with the maid. How could I trust her? Had I given her keys to the house? Didn't I feel that my privacy was being invaded by the maid? Wasn't I aware that given an inch, the maid would take a mile? Didn't I know that "they'" prefer to live in the shed out the back, that the maid was probably accepting my offer in order to avoid offending me?

Another argument often put forward goes like this: Most Africans prefer to work for expatriates rather than the local elite for the simple reason that they will benefit from better working conditions. It follows that many expats take it for granted that one should not be "too soft'" with staff. "You have to keep them in check" is the unspoken strategy. It is important to maintain the barriers and reinforce that strong sense of otherness – even among colleagues. Local staff who work for a foreign organisation will carry on living in their own homes, far from the expats' part of town. The distance and social disparity between the two neighbourhoods often lays bare any hope of mixing or intertwining the lives of the staff. At home, local staff might be without electricity and running water. The two groups only share space when they are at work, where teams have access to computers, the Internet, telephones, walkie-talkies and mobile phones. The two-tier system runs across virtually every aspect of life, including holidays, for example. Many foreign organizations – including the UN and the BBC – have a two-tier salary system as well: local staff are paid "local wages". They watch foreigners come to their country, receive very high salaries, take long holidays, drive around in four-by-fours with chauffeurs... while they carry on living off low salaries, which "compared to most jobs" are really quite good.

Some people argue today that what aid agencies are good at is emergency work. There's clearly a good case to be made in defence of food distribution programmes, for instance in the circumstances created by the conflict in Sudan's western region of Darfur. But even in emergency situations, not all aid workers work by the same rules. Most agencies pull their staff out of an area if their lives are threatened, and in Darfur certain aid agencies have done just that. What we hear about less is that often – not always – when NGOs pull out staff, they are referring only to foreign staff. Meanwhile, local staff remain on base because the area in which they are working is often the area where they live, where they were born and where they have spent much of their life.

For example, towards the end of the Angolan war, the city of Malange in the centre of the country became the target of fairly consistent shelling by rebels from the National Union for the Total Independence of Angola (UNITA). Many displaced people had already fled to the city from unprotected villages that had been targeted by rebel and government soldiers. Consequently, there were also a lot of aid agencies in Malange, providing aid to the displaced groups. However, when the UNITA shelling began in earnest, the NGOs pulled out. In other words, they removed all foreign staff working in the city. Most agencies completely closed down operations, leaving local staff without a job or salary. Others left a skeletal office in operation, run by local staff, who carried on working throughout the bombing campaigns. Some Angolans carried out the most heroic acts, working day in, day out to provide aid to people who had lost practically everything. Meanwhile, their expatriate colleagues were safe back in Luanda or out of the country entirely. Double standards? It would seem so: A sort of apartheid policy in liberal clothes.

Given the institutionalised discrimination practised by many foreign organisations working in Africa and elsewhere, it is no wonder that some staff – such as our party-goers on their treasure hunt – exploit local people for their own entertainment.

Notes

[1] www.usaid.gov/about_usaid/

[2] Italy's record is even worse: about 90 per cent of Italian aid ends up benefiting Italian "experts" and businesses.

[3] Net aid to Africa in 2002 was slightly more than $22 billion, including $1 billion from Britain and $2 billion from France. See Organisation for Economic Development **www.oecd.org**

[5] Roy, Arundhati (2004), "Public Power in the Age of Empire", Social Worker Online, 3 September. **www.socialistworker.org**

8

ACTIVISTOCRACY

Achal Prabhala

One day in January 2004, a group of excited schoolchildren from Mumbai entered a room at the WSF – the World Social Forum. The sign outside said "Rainbow Planet" and their teacher vaguely imagined that it promised crayons, colouring books and world peace. Instead, this particular group found itself confronted by the love that once dared not speak its name, whereupon the teacher blushed and fled, dragging her curious wards with her.

Imagine whirled peas. As Mumbai girded its loins for WSF, I was agog with excitement. It was my very first, and I had been looking forward to it for months. It was also the only WSF I could afford to attend, being as it was in my own backyard. I came, I saw, I wanted to be conquered. But all I got was a lungful of dust.

When my sister and I arrived at the WSF, we had no idea that it would be spread over 65 acres of land, or that there would be one hundred thousand others of our kind. We asked if wheelchairs were available (my sister is physically disabled). After some hours of hanging around, it became apparent that they were not. My cousin found us seats in a van. We cut a swathe through the common people trudging to the main stage, discovering to our horror that we were in an ambulance equipped with a wailing siren and rotating lights.

It deposited us in the VIP section – a small patch of grass right in front of the stage, cordoned off by tight security, presumably, for the activistocracy to mingle uninhibitedly. And they did. Arundhati Roy had a flower in her hair. The folks who made up Junoon rolled in, all black jeans, long hair and lit cigarettes, every bit the

Pakistani sufi-rock band of the moment. The show got on its way.

Junoon's performance was received ecstatically; their throaty rendition of *Sayonee* was just the thing to connect a hundred thousand individuals itching for love and revolution. Things went downhill thereon, with the usual lurid exhibitions of ancient culture. All in line with that famous rule of international activism: any act of resistance must involve ethnic people singing, clapping and swaying their hips.

Once the WSF began, however, I was grateful for any hipswaying that could tear me away me from crucial debates between crypto-autonomists and anarcho-syndicalists or whatever – especially when it was from sexuality activists like the folks at Rainbow Planet. These folks took their fun seriously, thank God, disregarding the quaint "days of war/ nights of love" protocol on offer. If there was a useful merging of the old left and the new left, it was primarily because of them.

These were some of the good bits.

At the plenary sessions, a mixture of bedlam and boredom prevailed. I'm not saying that it wasn't sweet of Mary, Trevor, Joe, Gilberto and Mustafa to trek all the way to Mumbai; I just wish I could have heard what they had to say. In the front rows, respectable activists and dilettantes strained their ears to hear about ethical globalisation, post-apartheid Soweto, bad IMF, good Brazil and the situation in Palestine. All we got was ambient clutter and a few muffled squeaks.

I missed hearing Leila Khaled, the Palestinian activist and celebrity hijacker. Friends had been immensely moved by her talk, so I read her up, first in a weirdly reverential interview for a trade magazine called *Aviation Security International*, and then on the BBC. While she came across as extremely warm, I did wonder about her outrage at being coshed, back then in 1970, and waking up to find her companion dead ("I was furious, shouting and crying") – given that they had been overpowered, after all, while trying to hijack a plane.

In the back rows, exclusively populated by the Indian

proletariat, people wondered when the Tamil and Hindi translation they had been promised was going to start. When it became clear that it wasn't going to happen, and that no one could hear anything anyway, they stretched out and sensibly fanned themselves to sleep. It was a good thing that the masses got some rest. There was so much for them to do.

Every time a camera crew came by, the masses had to march and shout "Down down World Bank!" or, alternatively, "Down down Coca-Cola!" University-educated researchers analysed the plight of oppressed people at panels; oppressed people, on the other hand, provided something that was quaintly billed as "testimonials." Meanwhile, fearless leaders were interviewed by equally fearless journalists in the air-conditioned media centre, which doubled up as a VIP clubhouse and offered e-mail access, gratis, to the chosen.

On the positive side, one of the nicest things about WSF Mumbai was that it was not MR – Mumbai Resistance – a sideshow that had fallen down across the road. The brainchild of some twisted little Stalinists, MR's beef with the WSF was that it had been tricked into believing that class was not the only valid unit of social analysis, thereby inviting the revolution to be led astray by feminists, queer people and what have you. MR broadcast its every indignant wheeze via a pseudo-academic mouthpiece – where it was deduced, in an earlier scholarly work, that abstract art was a CIA plot to distract the masses.

The other nice thing about the WSF is that there is no Plan. And the funniest thing about there being no Plan is that it endlessly consternates the nice Washingtonians and their tropical satellites who constitute the internal critique. No liberal, especially one who is actually at the WSF, wants to be publicly against it. (The most curious thing about the WSF might be that Nobel prize-wining economists are its most curious participants). They try to look like they're listening, all the while sighing inwardly, and I actually feel sorry for them. They appear to be gently probing for a quantifiable outcome, say, a 13% increase in total global desire for revolution. What they really mean is, Damn it why can't you just do as you're told?

But I digress. Who is the ideal WSF participant? She is a woman born and raised in an obscure rural part of any third world country, subjected to crushing poverty which forces her to migrate to the city. She gets a job on the shop floor, sewing buttons by day, decoding bootleg translations of Gramsci by night. Thus emboldened, she realises that power is simultaneously diffused and concentrated in Empire (the title of Hardt & Negri's first bestselling book). Persevering on, and having left the shop floor to "organise" she finds out that the answer to everything is Multitude (the title of their second bestselling book). Then, if she is truly deserving, she lands a job with a proper international NGO, corresponds with Susan George on e-mail and confers with Subcommondante Marcos in remote mountain hideaways. Finally, to crown her ascent to the ne plus ultra of activism (and now that she has an address recognised by the postal service), she uses her official credit card to pre-order the next Hardt & Negri manual on Amazon.com.

Two years after WSF Mumbai, I bumped into an altogether different kind of WSF participant in Orange Farm, a township near Johannesburg. I was at a celebration for International Women's Day and George had been temporarily employed by the organisers. He fondly recalled his trip to Mumbai, a week's stay at The President, a five-star deluxe hotel in the smartest part of town, and scratched his head over the alleged rape of a South African activist by a South African judge – a less than ideal fluid exchange that had dominated headlines in India at the time (the charge was subsequently withdrawn).

George was the kind of person who was grateful for any employment that came his way. He lived in a tin shack in a particularly desperate part of Orange Farm, and had been trying to get a regular job for years. I tallied the cost of his WSF jaunt – about US$3000.

I was reminded of a sentence I'd been hearing a lot lately. "Float like a butterfly, sting like a bee."

For a brief while this was the official motto of the Multitude, the masses pouncing on it as gritty Muhammad Ali, and radical intellectuals claiming it as pure Spinoza.

Certainly, it is the definitive WSF sound byte – a rousing combination of depth and clarity with an interpretive sweep to boot. Right at that moment though, it sounded quite silly.

Sure, I realise that instigating planetary revolution is a thankless career, and I won't pretend I have a clue as to how to go about it myself. Some of my best friends attend the WSF, and I firmly believe that everyone is entitled to some sex and tourism with their development. I just don't think that we should confuse the WSF for something that it isn't.

There have been many WSFs since my time in Mumbai: a round of "polycentric" meetings in 2006 that left participants somewhat confused, and a controversial one in Nairobi in 2007, which left many thoroughly disgusted. Yet, the movement shows no signs of backing down. Soon enough, the well-heeled indignant will meet in some salubrious location and declare that "another world is possible" – again.

But as they wonder why their masses are not fully down with the floating and stinging programme, they might learn to engage a little more equally with the loves and lives of the human beings whose interests they so tenderly protect.

9

A CAPITALIST CARNIVAL

Onyango Oloo

An Orwellian invasion was witnessed in Kenya during the World Social Forum (WSF) in January 2007. Kenyans saw an anti-globalisation event brought to them by a regional telecommunications behemoth, a pro-poor platform privatised by a profiteering "camilla of consultants" (to borrow one choice expression), an international event happening in Kenya, but locking out thousands of Kenyans, a capitalist carnival valorizing the business interests of a notorious Internal Security Minister with a past tainted by torture allegations, a civil society gathering dominated by an elite drawn from top-flight non-governmental organisations (NGOs), and a jamboree seared into the collective memory more for the hawking of African textiles and curios rather than for sustaining political engagement and mobilising the popular classes against the nefarious forces of neo-liberalism.

It may appear surreal that the hands keying in these words belong to someone who was in the thick of it all, amid the din, at the centre of the kitchen known as the Secretariat of the WSF Nairobi 2007 Organising Committee. To that extent, I was one of the mad cooks who whipped up the strange broth that left such a sour taste in many an activist's mouth.

One thing is clear: another world will never be possible as long as the process is driven by cynical NGO-types who are adept at hijacking and co-opting the ideals, struggles and aspirations of real social movements. That possible world will remain an unrealised dream as long as the WSF remains an annual jamboree of navel-gazing, self-referencing civil society globe-trotters.

One of the main claims of the World Social Forum is that

127

it is "an open space" where social actors map out real economic, social, cultural, political and other alternatives to the corporate status quo.

At WSF Nairobi 2007, the space was anything but open. A clique of arrogant and elitist powermongers – with a distinguished past in the trenches of anti-neocolonial struggles – managed to ensure that they excluded and marginalised a very large chunk of the very social forces that were supposed to be at the heart of the WSF 2007 process. Those excluded ranged from the bulk of the Secretariat itself (starting with someone like myself who was on paper one of the key actors) to inhabitants of Nairobi's informal settlements and Kenya's impoverished and marginalised rural communities.

In the meantime, these same civil society heavyweights traversed the world visiting capitals in the North and in the South mouthing platitudes about social justice, debt eradication, gender equality, youth empowerment, environmental protection, cultural and minority rights, and so on.

Here are a few snapshots:

The Kenya Social Forum, a component of the WSF 2007 Organising Committee, is an umbrella body of over 15 civil society groups and social movements. One of the most strident demands from the Kenyan NGO sector was for "transparency, accountability and good governance", an increasingly clichéd troika of criteria used to hold the feet of government officials to the fire. In the Kenyan context, corruption has been adjudged as among the top ailments afflicting the country. Yet during the WSF event in Nairobi, a tendering committee drawn from these very same civil society bodies presided over a bizarre procurement process that saw tenders being "won" by some of the individuals sitting on the very same tendering committee!

Another case in point. Coca Cola and its blood-stained products were banned from the WSF space and hawking of products by big multinationals was frowned upon by the organisers. Yet in Nairobi the entire event had at least one corporate sponsor – Kenya's second largest mobile operator, Celtel. A five-star hotel outlet owned by the country's notorious law and order minister was allocated prime space by local organisers who were once tortured by the Kenyan government. Another five-star hotel long seen as a bastion of racist colonial settlers in the pre-independence period and a major fund raiser for the state of Israel in the 1970s also had star billing at WSF Nairobi 2007.

One of the enduring themes of the World Social Forum is world peace and the struggle against militarism. Yet the gates at Kasarani Sports Complex, the venue of WSF Nairobi 2007, were manned by rifle-wielding paramilitary and police personnel who threw bewildered Kenyan attendees into the police post at the venue because a section of the organising committee had directed that no one should enter the venue without a name tag – which one could only receive after paying a hefty entrance fee, which many of the Kenyan participants could not afford.

Surely among the most sickening attributes of the Nairobi event was the open disdain displayed by some of the organisers for elements drawn from the wretched of the earth who were supposed to be the subjects and actors of WSF 2007, with one high profile member of the Organizing Committee dismissing the protesting masses as "glue sucking urchins from Korogocho (a slum in Nairobi)."

Many of these negative tendencies can be directly linked to the dominant role that NGOs – as opposed to social movements – played in the preparations for the WSF Nairobi event.

James Petras proved pretty prescient in his late 1990s analysis of NGOs in the Southern context:

NGOs emphasise projects, not movements; they "mobilise" people to produce at the margins but not to struggle to control the basic means of production and wealth; they focus on technical financial assistance of projects, not on structural conditions that shape the everyday lives of people. The NGOs co-opt the language of the left: "popular power," "empowerment," "gender equality," "sustainable development," "bottom-up leadership." The problem is that this language is linked to a framework of collaboration with donors and government agencies that subordinates practical activity to non-confrontational politics. The local nature of NGO activity means that "empowerment" never goes beyond influencing small areas of social life, with limited resources, and within the conditions permitted by the neoliberal state and macroeconomy.[1]

Kenya's social movements have had a long and chequered history, beginning with anti-colonial struggles in the decades preceding independence, and reaching a crescendo during the struggle for Kenya's "second liberation" from dictatorship in the 1980s and 1990s. In 2002, when Kenyan voters turned up in their millions at the polling booths to throw out a highly unpopular 24-year old regime, civil society organisations were part of the bedrock of the opposition. It was expected that with a new government in place, many of the precepts preached by NGOs would form part of the DNA of the new regime. Hopes were raised when some prominent members of civil society actually romped into power as Members of Parliament, before they were appointed to the Cabinet and offered plum government positions. Instead of the much anticipated "change from within", what we saw was more of the same – former key civil society actors becoming mired in new cases of corruption and abuse of office.

This leads me to argue that the line between the "State" and "civil society" is a blurred one. There is really no rationale to suggest that ethically the latter is superior to the former, or vice versa.

Flowing from the above, I firmly believe that those of us who are in civil society should climb down from our high horses and do some introspecting on how, wittingly or unwittingly, we are so routinely implicated as accomplices in perpetrating crimes against the poor, the voiceless and the marginalised – the very constituencies that we claim to be fighting and dying for. We must reassess our relationship with big overseas funders and Western nations that ultimately bankroll our activities via the international donor agencies and foundations from which we seek sustenance.

One should also hasten to add that not all civil society organisations and NGOs fall into one neat basket. There are just as many NGOs seeking common cause with the oppressed as there are NGOs morphing into corporate-like octopuses. But perhaps, as some of my more radical friends argue, it is time to step away from the NGOs and revert to the grassroots social movements where real social transformation takes place.

Notes

[1] **James Petras,** *Imperialism and NGOs in Latin America, 1997*

10

THE GOOD HOUSE NEGRO

Philip Ochieng

---

*The Negro is a child, and with children nothing can be done
without the use of authority...With regard to Negroes, then, I
have coined the formula: I am your brother, it is true, but your
elder brother.*

– **Dr. Albert Schweitzer, 1921**

For most of the last five hundred years, Europe – the
world's economic, strategic and intellectual overlord
– has depicted the black person as less than human,
a being that has only enough brains to serve as a beast of
burden in the white man's industries, plantations and
homes. Negritude – a tri-continental force dedicated to
reasserting the black person's presence and vitality –
blossomed among black students in Western Europe and
North America in the first half of the 20th century as a
rejoinder to Caucasian racism in historiography, science,
anthropology, literature, sociology and other forms of
intellectual expression. As a mental self-liberation
movement, the Negritudists purported to produce works
that equalled those of white artists in excellence and
message – in *haute couture,* cuisine, song, dance,
instrumentation, theatre, poetry, sculpture, painting,
journalism, architecture and other fine arts.

But what exactly was Negritude's ideological-moral
content? What is its proper place in the history of
thought? An answer was supplied by Dundusu Chisiza in
an article in which the Malawian writer divided human
beings into three broad race-based mental categories.
According to him, the Western ("white") man excelled in

science and industry; the Eastern ("yellow") man in occult mysticism and the Southern ("black") man in "humanism". In other words, these attributes were basically racial or genetic (not merely cultural). Similarly, Negritude held that the human trichotomy was inborn and permanent.

Modern knowledge shows, however, that all human societies – of all skin colours — are characterised simultaneously by humanism, mysticism, technology and science. The greater the techno-scientific level, the deeper the consciousness and the less the mysticism. At the same time, however, the more this is so, the more the aristocracy of each society seeks to preserve mysticism as a means of keeping the masses in their place. That is why the greater the material gap in a society, the less humanistic the upper classes. This is a cultural process, not a racial one, and only those with a vested interest in its material and intellectual lopsidedness can seek to clothe it in racial garments.

Thus Africans are no more humane in their natural make-up than are Yankees or Britons. If, in Chisiza's time, Africans showed more "humanism" than did Europeans, it was not because of any gene. It was only because they had only recently emerged from the extended family system. This primitive communism was what Tanzania's Julius Nyerere – as if trying to reinvent the wheel – tried to resume as *Ujamaa*, not realising that Westerners had emerged from their *Ujamaa* many millennia earlier before reaching their present level of ruthless individualism.

But, as if to show that race has nothing to do with it, the introduction of European capitalism in Africa, not much more than a century and a half ago, has produced an African individual every bit as greedy, as go-getting, as aggressive, as cruel as Genghis Khan and the Sicilian Mafioso. That was what happened to "oriental mysticism" as soon as China, Japan, Singapore, South Korea and India put industry on a pedestal. Who today can assert that, against the Indians, the Japanese and the Far Eastern city-states, the Westerner excels in science and technology as a matter of genetics?

Petit bourgeois radicalism

What is fast banishing mysticism is the same force that once expelled its Orphic, Hermetic and other forms from the Mediterranean world. Barbara Wootton and Richard Dawkins comment that science has a way of removing mysteries, bit by bit, from the divine's face to expose him for what he is. In a *Sunday Nation* polemic in 1966, group editor-in-chief George Githii attacked the self-denigration in the attitudes of post-colonial, educated black people who resorted to such terms as "Africanism" and "Negritude" to try to depict the black person as genetically different from the white, the brown and the yellow. This essentially reactionary philosophy includes *Ujamaa* (Julius Nyerere), "African socialism" (Tom Mboya) and Negritude. (The founders and principal exponents of Negritude were francophone Africans influenced by French Surrealism; they included Aime Cesaire, Leopold Sedar Senghor, Okot p'Bitek and the editors of Dakar's *Presence Africaine*, especially Alioune Diop – all labelled as *Orphees Noirs* or "Black Orpheuses" by the French philosopher Jean-Paul Sartre.)

At best, these philosophies represent what Marxists would call petit bourgeois radicalism. As Nyerere learnt when he tried to execute a "revolution" by means of the peasantry and *vibwanyenye* (urban traders), petit bourgeois radicalism always, in the end, proves counterrevolutionary. At worst, Negritude, in particular, is an abject intellectual surrender to European racism; it asserts that there is something that may be called *"negrum"* which, being innate in black people, forces them to do things peculiarly differently from the rest of humanity.

That, at any rate, is precisely what one means whenever one talks of, for instance, "African socialism." It is like talking of "African physics" or "African mathematics." Wrote Githii: "... Senghor ... bases [his 'African socialism'] ... on what he calls the *African theory of knowledge*." That was the crux of the matter. The Negritudists taught that the black person is governed by an epistemology different from the white man's – that is to say, exactly the same doctrine as was taught by every 19th-century European anthropologist.

135

Senghor was categorical. The African "... thinks like one of those Third Day Worms — a pure field of sensations." Said he: "The vital force of the Negro African [is] his surrender to the object. [It is not] animated by reason..." In other words, the African reacts only in accordance with the common-sense information which his eyes, ears, nose, skin and taste buds bring to him from any object of outer nature. As Jean Piaget informs us in his book *Psychology and Epistemology*, the immediate composition of these senses is what is called *perception*. Thus the African is capable only of perception. But all animals and some plants (like the mimosa) are capable of this kind of "thinking". If this is all that the African person can manage, then the African is no better than a horse, a dog, a chimp, a gorilla or a porpoise in his mentality.

For the Caucasian, however, this common-sense or inward information passes through certain nerves to a brain centre where it is processed and turned into logico-mathematical data which he then turns back upon the object from which the raw information originally came. This outward or subjective process is what is called conception (as opposed to mere perception) because, through it, the Caucasian is able to use the logico-mathematical data to impute other (real or imaginary) qualities to that object. These imputed qualities are what prod him to seek to examine the object more closely – for instance, subjecting it to measurements or laboratory experiments – with a view to changing it to meet certain human needs. In a word, conception is the basis of all science and technology.

But, because the black person can never go beyond perception, he is incapable of conception and, therefore also of reasoning and of science and technology. Statements like this were made by such celebrated white scholars as David Hume, Georg WF Hegel, George Trevelyan, Hugh Trevor-Roper and recently, one James Watson. But that precisely was what Dundusu Chisiza – a man as black as charcoal – also said.

In *Religion of the Southern Luo*, Okot p'Bitek avers repeatedly that Africa's salvation lies, not in science or technology or industry, but only in "culture." It lies only in returning to the primitive gadgets and mumbo jumbo of our ancestors. It did not occur to the Negritudists that, under protracted and extreme oppression, the oppressed group turns more and more to "feeling" and "emotion" as its chief planks in argument. For the oppressed person's reasoning power has been suppressed for so long that it has gone dormant.

Ali Mazrui writes that if you are to take pride in such backwardness, you are resigned to inferiority. "The civilised people," writes he, "were supposed to be those who built castles, palaces and fortresses. As a black primitivist confessed with pride, 'My Negritude (my blackness) is no tower and no cathedral; it delves into the deep, red flesh of the soil.'"

There is a great deal of mental lethargy to be found both in the colonised African as well as in the enslaved "Negro" – always accompanied by religious over-enthusiasm and such other "emotional" pursuits as music and sex — so that the oppressor soon theorises that this is the "natural" attribute of the victim. After a long period of that theorising, the victim himself begins to believe it. That, in a nutshell, is the story of Negritude.

"Africans don't hate that way"

Many black Americans, steeped in romanticism about Africa, on first landing on African soil and watching the elaborate welcoming rituals, marvel at the display of "soul". In this way, they believe they are breaking away from the white man's attitude towards Africa, when, in fact, they are only confirming Europe's view of Africa as a place whose inhabitants are capable only of things of the "soul" and never of things of the brain.

But it is not only black Americans who succumb to this self-denigration. Surrealism, an art movement of the 1920s, used evocative juxtaposition of incongruous images in order to introduce unconscious or dream elements in art. "The realist attitude, inspired by positivism ... has for me an air that is hostile to all intellectual and moral achievement," wrote André Breton, the "pope" of the

Surrealists. According to the painter Hans Arp, Surrealism "...aimed to destroy the reasonable deceptions of man and recover the natural and unreasonable order." To that extent, then, surrealism rejected all the social liabilities of capitalist society but was unable to identify capitalism as the ultimate cause of those liabilities. Therefore, instead of fighting capitalism, the Surrealists sought to flee from it.

Not only was the movement as characteristically irrational as Negritude, its African offshoot, it also, like Negritude, represented a surrender to the world as seen by the very same establishment from which the Surrealists were trying to run away. Just as they "rejected" bourgeois society but, in trying to flee it, only found themselves surrendering to it by a roundabout route, so the Negritudists, by "rejecting" white racism, only succeeded in surrendering to it through the back door.

We have seen that here, in East Africa. Chisiza and p'Bitek, while purporting to assert their Africanness in the face of European insolence, merely fell into the trap. Kenyan theologian John Mbiti evinces it again and again. In his *African Religions and Philosophy*, the professor elevates European thought as "logical, reflexive and personal," and relegates African thought to "intuitive, personal and a lived experience."

Hence, Africans, because they excel in the field of sympathy and human relations, are incapable of hating with as much passion as Caucasians, as the American journalist David Lamb discovered when he interviewed Sam Weller, a one-time soldier, farmer and professional hunter who worked as the manager of an exclusive country club in the Aberdare Forest, the site of the most brutal attacks by British colonialists against Kenya's Mau Mau movement in the 1950s. In his book titled *The Africans*, Lamb recounts his conversation with Weller:

Sam Weller was a young British army captain when Mau Mau terrorist attacks began, and his men spent many months in the Aberdare Forest trying to track down and capture or kill General Ndirang'u. "I had the old boy in my sights a couple of times," chuckled Weller, who manages the Aberdare

Country Club and employs Ndirang'u as his driver. "But he always managed to slip away ... Really, though, unless a visitor like yourself brings it up, you don't hear anyone, black or white, talk about the Mau Mau any more up here. It was so long ago.

"Why has it been forgotten? Well, partly I think, because the African isn't capable of the depth of emotion that the European has. He doesn't love his women or hate his enemies with the same intensity. You look at a good solid white hatred and it can last for generations. Africans don't hate that way."[1],

Here, an old colonial hand admits, but very cleverly, that what he once did to Africans was atrocious. He wonders at his luck that Africans do not hate him for it with as much intensity as "Europeans" would have under the same circumstances. Amazingly, he does not see that the transformation of Ndirang'u from a rebellious "field negro" to a "good house negro" is nothing short of miraculous.[2]

Another example of this liberalist stereotyping: In his autobiography *A Love Affair with the Sun*, Sir Michael Blundell, a liberal colonial farmer and politician, writes:

Fifteeen years [after the Mau Mau outbreak in 1952] I was sitting near [Jomo] Kenyatta at a passing-out parade of Kenya Air Force cadets. Alongside me was a short portly Kikuyu, well-dressed in a blue suit and a pronounced stomach that denoted good living. He kept looking at me, making small exclamations and then examining me once again. At last he leaned towards me and said, "What is your name. I seem to know your face very well." I gave him my name, whereupon his face broke into an enormous smile followed by gurgles of laughter.

He leaned over again and said, "Do you know, 15 years ago I vowed to kill you; we were going to garrotte you, in the Rugong Forest, and here you are!" "Yes," I said, "You weren't very successful, were you? What are you doing now?" "Oh," he replied, "I am all right, I am the owner of the Oyster Prairie Bar in Nakuru." And we settled down amicably side by side to watch the proceedings. I reflected that there can be few people who have met and enjoyed a laugh and reminiscence with their would-be assassin. This little tale to me shows the spirit of modern Kenya, and the attitudes that have contributed to its stability.[3]

Blundell's story is exactly the same as that of Sam Weller, except that Blundell, being a more intelligent reporter, does not seek to give the "forgiveness" a racial interpretation. It belongs purely to the historico-political circumstances in which Kenya had achieved independence.

"Forgiveness" was a foregone conclusion under a class that was so ready to give in completely to neo-colonial interests, given the fact that Kenyatta, a representative of the nascent black bourgeoisie, had totally surrendered to the sop of political liberalism. In retrospect, then, Kenyatta's "forgive-and-forget" attitude is quite understandable. That Kenyatta appears as being "magnanimous" to the white settlers was inevitable after the false identification of him as the organiser and chief leader of Mau Mau, that truly *passionate* movement.

Lamb, who spent four years in Africa in the early 1980s as the bureau chief for the *Los Angeles Times*, complains about the apparent submissive and forgiving nature of the African:

In many ways, the longer I stayed in Africa, the less I really understood the nuances of the African character, and any Westerner who says he feels differently is probably being less than honest. Before going to Africa, I had lived many years in Asia and for two in Australia, and when I left those continents, I felt I had a grasp of who the people were, how they would react to certain situations, why they respond in particular ways, what they thought about the world around them.

But the African often becomes a deepening mystery. It is rare that he will reveal his inner emotions or talk about his beliefs in more than superficial terms. As often as not, he will tell you what he thinks you want to hear rather than risk offending you with an opinionated view. He does not often defy authority and he will follow anyone who asserts himself as a leader, however inept, with an amazing alacrity. His resilience extends beyond any logical human limits; his crops can fail, his children can die, his government can treat him grievously and the African still carries on, uttering no protest, sharing no complaints.[4]

As an African who has taken part in numerous mass protests and often missed a bullet by a whisker ever since I was a stripling, I can only express astonishment. This man says Africans won their independence in battlefields and, in the same breath, that Africans take all oppression with total resignation.

Emotional numbness

The deification of Kenyatta — of which even the Kenyan author Ngugi wa Thiong'o is guilty in his early novels — led most Kenyans to accept Kenyatta's teaching just before independence that we should (forgive and) forget all the brutalities the white man had inflicted on our skins and minds, our hearts and our lands. Kenyatta pleaded with Europeans to continue and even intensify their ruthless economic exploitation of Africans in a situation where the Ndirang'us now had no choice but to forgive and forget the past.

Thus encouraged, the whites streamed back into Africa to reintroduce an even more insidious form of racism, the subtle and paternalistic kind, and the African elite continued tacitly to accept that white people know what is good for Africa. The result is that many who cannot find jobs in their own countries now occupy important jobs in African capitals – in industry, tourism, marketing, manufacturing and even football management – while qualified Africans are denied such jobs. Meanwhile, in Europe and in America, direct racism is rearing its ugly head again against blacks, Arabs, Indians, Turks, Chinese and Filipinos. In recent years, this racism has been maintained by an intellectual and emotional numbness, a fatal incapacity to have any feelings for non-white people, unless these feelings are cloaked in words such as "charity" or "aid". This numbness has been made worse by George Bush's "war on terror", which has added another nigger to the pile: the Muslim male.

Commenting on this aspect of Negritude, Ali Mazrui notes: "Of course negritude and other social schools of African romantic thought have their African critics as well as their converts. Ezekiel Mphahlele, the South African writer, was among the earliest black rebels against the pristine assumptions of negritude. Mphahlele believes that when Negritude assumes too much innocence it cannot at the same time attribute to [the] African man the capacity for natural spontaneity. After all, to be spontaneous sometimes implies reacting in violent ways."

As we know, although black violence against Boer violence was, at the beginning, spontaneous, during the time of "Zik" – as we called him when he taught African literature at the University of Nairobi in the mid-1960s — the anti-apartheid movement in South Africa had become well-organised and conscious. More relevantly, it was being carried out through methodical and well-calculated violence. Mphahlele was part of that movement, a movement that totally belies Lamb's allegation that Africans always tolerate oppression with equanimity. As Mazrui recalls, Mphahlele tossed the following remarkable words like a bombshell at an Africanist conference in Dakar in 1963:

> I do not accept... the way in which too much of the poetry inspired by Negritude romanticises Africa – as a symbol of innocence, purity and artless primitiveness. I feel insulted when some people imply that Africa is not also a violent continent. I am a violent person, and proud of it, because it is often a healthy state of mind ... Some day I am going to plunder, rape, set things on fire; I am going to cut someone's throat; I am going to subvert the government; I am going to organise a *coup d'etat*. Yes, I am going to oppose my own people; I am going to hunt down the rich fat black men who bully the small weak black men and destroy them: I am going to become a capitalist, and woe to all those who cross my path or who want to be my servants or chauffeurs and so on...I am going to lead a breakaway church – there is money in it. I am going to attack the black bourgeoisie while I cultivate a garden, rear dogs and parrots; listen to jazz and classics, read

"culture" and so on. Yes, I am also going to organise a strike. Don't you know that sometimes I kill to the rhythm of drums and cut the sinews of a baby to cure it of paralysis?

"Zik" was, in fact, one of the most cultured men that I ever met: gentle, soft-spoken and keenly conscious of good taste. But speaking at a conference dominated by Negritudists at a time when black romanticism – inspired by Gallic surrealism — was on the ascendancy, he was quite justified to "explode" in this fashion to remind Africans that they are full human beings who, at a time of vulgarity, cruelty and violence, will also react with violence, vulgarity and cruelty.

These are things — extremely unfortunate though they are – that human beings do all the time to other human beings as a result of the appallingly lopsided way in which we share power and wealth. When you confront a slave or a colonised person with the litany, day after day, for five centuries, that he is a good-for-nothing, he eventually comes to believe it and to seek other, often irrational ways, of expressing his humanity. Under the rabid individualist pursuits introduced to us by colonialism and now being maintained by neo-colonialism, such inhumanity and such reactions to it will continue throughout the world.

Europeans do not proclaim their "Euritude" for the simple reason that, as a race, Europeans have not in recent centuries been enslaved on account of their race. There is no need to announce that "White is Beautiful." Self-evidently, all human skin colours are beautiful. And no black or yellow conqueror has ever asserted that white is ugly.

The urge to assert tribal or racial beauty and vitality is usually the activity of the intellectuals of tribes and races long oppressed and long denied the means of self-survival, self-dignity and self-expression. But – as we have seen here – such assertions are often completely wrongheaded. Often they merely reaffirm the myths created by the oppressor about the real character of the oppressed.

Negritude was the affirmation that the black person was excellent in the mental cocoon that the oppressor allotted to him. Shorn of its intellectual wrapping — such as Aime

Cesaire's sublime poetry — Negritude was no more than self-degradation, self-denigration, self-surrender to every form of insolence that the white man has heaped upon the black person for centuries. Feminist writer Andrea Dworkin aptly described this form of masochism as "the bewildering resignation and self-destructive impassivity of those who are hurt, maimed in fact, by social cruelty and intimate brutality".

Notes

[1] Lamb, David (1984), *The Africans*, New York: Vintage.

2 Malcolm X defined a "house negro" as a slave who "loves his master more than he loves himself" and a "field negro" as a slave who "hates his master".

[3] Blundell, Michael (1994), *A Love Affair with the Sun*, Nairobi: Kenway Publications.

[4] Lamb,1984.

Part 3:
THE POLITICS OF AID

11

MEN BEHAVING BADLY

Sunny Bindra

The hand that receives is always below the hand that gives.
– African proverb

The President of Uganda began behaving badly in 2005. Yoweri Museveni successfully changed his country's constitution to allow him to run for a third presidential term in early 2006. He began muzzling the press in his country. He also locked up his main challenger and former personal physician, Dr. Kizza Besigye, on dubious charges of treason and rape.

The Right Honourable Hilary Benn, Britain's Secretary of State for International Development, sent Museveni a stern letter announcing the withholding of some of the development aid his country had lavished on Uganda since Museveni took power in the 1980s. Benn cited the imprisonment of Besigye and the use of government resources in campaigning for the ruling National Resistance Movement.

President Museveni went ballistic. In a widely published response, he lambasted the "donor" and "beggar" relationship between the West and Africa. He accused Britain of trying to exercise "suzerainty" over Uganda's "sovereign" issues. He mocked Mr. Benn for pointing out the fact that Britain had contributed £800 million to Uganda since 1986, claiming that the quantum of money received by Africa in aid paled into insignificance when compared with what it lost due to unfavourable terms of trade.

The president listed various forms of "meddling" by donors: in counter-terrorism; in interfering with state support of industrial enterprises; even in dam-building.

He asked Mr. Benn to "point out to me one single Black African country that has transitioned because of...aid from the West since Ghana's independence in 1957." And he finished with this conclusive remark: "What Uganda and Africa need most is independence in decision-making, not subservience, satellite status or dependency status."

What was most interesting about this ill-tempered exchange was that it did not involve one of Africa's notorious Big Men. Up to that point, Yoweri Museveni had been the aid industry's poster child, one of the "new breed of African leaders" that Britain and America had been hailing since the 1990s. Uganda was supposed to prove the argument once and for all: That aid given to the right countries in the right circumstances with the right conditions produces the right results. The country is estimated to have received $11 billion since 1987 – and the result, as we saw in 2005, is the pointing of fingers and the hurling of accusations and counter-accusations.

It makes you wonder, does it not, about the nature of this "relationship"? Both sides seem happy – one to bestow, the other to receive – until, for whatever reason, the flow is interrupted. Then the acrimony begins. Don't tell us how to run our lives, says one side. You're misusing our money and abusing our trust, says the other. Don't interfere in our affairs, shouts one. You happily took the money and blew it on parties, screams the other.

Meanwhile, in neighbouring Kenya, Sir Edward Clay, Britain's High Commissioner to the country (who had also served as Britain's High Commissioner to Uganda when Museveni was still the darling of Western donors) became famously undiplomatic in 2004 when he was so incensed by the failures of President Mwai Kibaki's NARC government to contain grand corruption that he likened the recipients of Her Majesty's aid money to "gluttons" who were now "vomiting on our shoes." He continued his outspoken campaign even after he left Kenya, railing against the World Bank's decision to resume aid to the country in 2006. In an open letter to the Bank's President, Paul Wolfowitz, he accused the institution of "adding to, not subtracting from, the sufferings of the peasantry." He asked the Bank to "sharpen up its political awareness" and to "avoid blind and offensive blundering."[1]

Should all this tetchiness surprise us? I don't think so. Even in ordinary life, relationships between givers and takers are always fraught with difficulty. As an example, consider this: at some stage in our lives many of us (especially those of us who live in Africa) have had to support disadvantaged friends or relatives. Where that exchange involves reasonable sums provided to overcome temporary difficulty, both sides are happy. The giver basks in the glow of philanthropy or duty; the recipient is grateful for the kindness shown at a time of need.

It all goes horribly and predictably wrong, however, if the dependency continues indefinitely. Once the kind-hearted, socially responsible one has been doling out large sums for many years and the needy, dependant one has been pocketing them, the recriminations begin. The giver will start to notice that the beggar he's supporting does not seem to have as frugal a lifestyle as one should expect in the circumstances. He begins to question the dependant's efforts to reduce his dependence. He starts handing out lectures about how he works hard for his money, and how he should not have to pay for the laziness or poor judgement of others.

The recipient has no choice but to listen, but seethes with anger. He, in turn, looks at the giver's opulent lifestyle and rages at his mean-mindedness in withholding what must be small change for him. He resents being questioned about his efforts to secure his own income. He reminds the giver of the favours he has bestowed on his benefactor in times past. He dreams about the day when he will fling the money back in his tormentor's face.

Far from being productive or necessary, the donor-dependant relationship most often ends in mutual hatred. And amid the final acrimony, one crucial fact is forgotten: the longer the relationship has carried on, the less capable the dependant is of reducing his dependence. The years of being held up by another do take their toll: skills wither, and a loss of confidence grows insidiously. Even with all the taunting and goading he is subjected to, the dependant is not motivated to rise up and finally fend for himself: no, all he is able to think about is *switching donors*.

Whether it's between nations or individuals, the donor-dependant relationship weakens both sides. One side loses its kindness and tolerance; the other its dignity and self-respect. In the end, neither benefits. In the end, friendship and kinship are lost.

The aid charade

It is this basic aspect of human nature that is being forgotten in the aid debate. For too long, we have been misled into thinking many fallacious things: That poor countries (particularly African ones) cannot make it on their own; that rich countries owe some historical debt to the poor ones, and must therefore keep slipping them some money to alleviate their guilt; that more development money equals more growth; that development plans can be orchestrated from up above and far away; that poverty can be "made history" by the rich nations.

Fortunately, this conventional wisdom is increasingly under challenge. Joseph Stiglitz, winner of a Nobel Prize for economics, weighed in first with a stinging critique of the International Monetary Fund and the World Bank and the conditions they attach to development aid.[2] He asked for nothing less than an overhaul of the international financial framework that governs trade and aid.

William Easterly, a former World Bank economist, pointed out that after pumping in nearly $2.3 trillion in aid to developing countries, ostensibly to remove poverty, the West has little to show for the effort.[3] He rails against the idea that complex, utopian plans can be devised for poor countries from afar. He dismisses the efforts of foreign technocrats and aid workers as (mostly) well-intended meddling that has almost never had the desired effect of hauling nations out of crippling poverty.

Robert Calderisi, another former World Bank functionary, has written of the shortcomings and indulgences of foreign aid in Africa.[4] He asks the continent to take a hard look at its own problems and weaknesses, and writes damningly of the aid charade: "In trying to please aid officials, African countries feel debased, like circus dogs forced to perform tricks." One of his radical prescriptions is to cut direct aid to individual countries in Africa by half, arguing that less aid would force giver and taker to use it better.

Percy Mistry, an investment banker and Chairman of the Oxford International Group, tells us that Africa's problem is not a lack of *financial* capital (having received, and largely squandered, nearly $1 trillion [in 2005 dollars] in foreign aid since 1965), but a crippling shortage of *human* capital, the skills and expertise needed to take the continent onto a self-propelled growth trajectory.[5] Mistry believes that African countries must focus on their own resources by harnessing savings and investment capital while simultaneously investing in developing the right skill-sets for their economies.

These are thoughtful and forceful critiques. The prescriptions for change are also far-reaching and often radical. Yet to even get to an agenda for reform, one must begin with the psychological insight: Great harm is done to people when they are made dependent on others. The hand that receives will one day rise against the hand that gives, and vice versa.

Able-bodied beggars

Recently, when I wrote about Bill Gates and Warren Buffet and their remarkable initiatives in changing the world of philanthropy in my weekly column in Kenya's *Sunday Nation*, I was horrified to find my mailbox filled with pleas from Kenyans to connect them and their "projects" to the two great men so that they could solicit donations. At every level, this affliction reveals itself. Our governments attend global begging shops looking for "development aid". Our businessmen and women scour the globe seeking "investment capital" at preferential rates. Our NGOs work the international charity circuit, pleading for "operational funding". And able-bodied beggars line our roads, seeking their next meal to enable them to live to beg for another day. If this is not the same problem in different guises, I am missing something."[6]

Let the international aid game indeed reform itself. But the first thing to do is to break away from our own dependency. President Museveni took umbrage against the patronising attitude of the British, but why did he relegate his country to beggar status in the first place? Why did he accept a situation in which more than half of his country's budget was being financed by donors? Why did he stand by and allow his ministers to be dictated to about which roads to build, which sectors to invest in, and what laws to pass? When a hard-nosed operative like Museveni (who launched a successful guerrilla campaign against an oppressive regime) puts himself in the hands of the aid industry for so many years, we have reason to be worried. He only appears to have rediscovered Uganda's need for "sovereignty" once the money taps were turned off.

Self-reliance can be achieved. Kenya has made great financial strides in this regard, increasing its generation of tax revenues remarkably in recent years. It has harnessed its own capital sources, using the surplus funds of its own businesses and its Diaspora. It is successfully designing a long-term, homegrown economic growth plan that is aimed at reducing donor dependency and increasing self-sufficiency. Yet the aid habit is hard to kick. President Mwai Kibaki is still playing the donor-switching game, successfully wooing the Chinese and the Arabs to provide aid for projects when the traditional donors act coy. The deadening mindset is intact.

We will learn. A new generation of Africans is questioning the need to beg. We are beginning to realise that something that takes ten years to do with your own ideas and your own resources is superior to a three-year programme planned, funded and dictated by the IMF. We are waking up to the fact that we cannot always be unschooled bumpkins in someone else's flawed game; we must generate our own development, by ourselves and in our own way.

Africa's real problem has been the appalling leaders who have steered its path since the 1960s. The dearth of talent and ethics at the top has gone hand-in-hand with aid dependency. It is far easier for the ignorant, the unimaginative and the grasping to simply take the aid on offer, rather than engage in the much more difficult task of self-determined economic growth. And the donor community, to its discredit, has engaged in an unseemly waltz with Africa's incompetent and greedy leaders, occasionally going into a sulk and sitting out a dance, but always returning to the floor when the music changes. So, what then is the point of the angry and forceful words? Museveni may have accused the British of many things, but Uganda is still feeding at the aid trough. Britain may have had its footwear soiled by Kenyans, but it is still priming the pump. Both sides seem very comfortable with all the hypocrisy.

Homegrown development does occur: Indeed, history has always taught that it is the norm rather than the exception. William Easterly points out that the countries with the best per capita growth rates from 1980 to 2002 also had low dependency on foreign aid; the ten lowest-performing countries, on the other hand, were almost all heavily aid-reliant. More depressingly, almost all the countries in the former group were Asian; the countries that were poor and dependent were mostly African.

The countries that have transformed themselves have never been in the donors' high-dependency unit for long periods. They have used aid, yes; but judiciously and for limited periods. They have depended on themselves, empowered themselves and thought for themselves. Indeed, they have almost all come in for great criticism from the West: China, for being too authoritarian; Japan and South Korea, for their governments' penchant for intervening in their economies, and for favouring large conglomerates; India for pursuing its ambition to become a nuclear power. By and large, these countries have ignored the prescriptions from the rich countries and have charted their own paths.

True success in individual life rarely comes from being given a drip-feed of money and being led by the nose by a benefactor who doesn't understand you but is full of patronising advice. It comes from a personal sense of purpose, determination and clear thinking. Money tends to follow success, not to lead it. African leaders keep forgetting what they know to be true in their personal lives: At the end of the day, achievement comes from knowledge, enterprise and dedication to a cause, not from handouts.

Notes

1 Clay, Sir Edward (2006) "Open Letter to World Bank Boss", *Sunday Nation*, 29 January.
2 Stiglitz, Joseph (2002) *Globalization and its Discontents*. USA: W.W. Norton & Company.
3 Easterly, William (2006) *The White Man's Burden*. New York: The Penguin Press
4 Calderisi, Robert (2007) *The Trouble with Africa*. New Haven and London: Yale University Press.
5 Mistry, Percy S. (2005) "Reasons For Sub-Saharan Africa's Development Deficit", *African Affairs*, 23 September.
6 Bindra, Sunny (2006) "The Flip Side of Philanthropy", *Sunday Nation*, 20 August.

12

WHY AID HAS FAILED AFRICA SO SPECTACULARLY

Maina Mwangi

The relevance of aid to Africa cannot possibly be in doubt. Indeed, it is as relevant in its own way as Aids, civil war and famine are in theirs; it is one of the defining characteristics of Africa.

The picture that most people have of Africa is of a continent whose people – when not fighting each other in the most brutal manner possible, or dying in large numbers of preventable diseases like Aids and malaria, or showing up emaciated on the world's television screens – are constantly begging or demanding that the world help them.

The original thinking behind aid was surely good, in that it sought to help new nations to find their feet. This approach didn't last long. Aid was soon ideologised; the competing superpowers saw aid as a political tool, almost regardless of what it actually achieved in terms of economic and institutional growth. Thus Americans and their allies, and the Soviets and theirs, and (most notoriously of all) the French competed to finance ever more economically illiterate projects, or worse, to pretend that arms given to prop up their various nasty friends in Africa counted as "aid".

This is the point at which sensible African countries should have got off the habit. The entire aid industry is based on a demonstrable fallacy: that aid can stimulate economic growth. No country on earth has ever been developed solely by aid. It is frequently claimed that the Marshall Plan and its Japanese equivalent prove the opposite case. Now both are examples of remarkable wisdom and foresight, not to mention generosity. But aid to the defeated Axis powers cannot be looked at in isolation. There were certain factors that made aid a beneficial thing in Germany and Japan that do not exist in Africa. In spite of the aberrant behaviour of Hitler and Tojo, both countries had a recent history of *homegrown* industrialisation. Germany did not need aid to develop its enormous pre-war chemical and heavy engineering industries. That was done by entrepreneurs, often in spite of a primitive politics that saw the be-all and end-all of economic activity as the eventual military and political domination of other countries. The history of Japan is remarkably similar. The point is that the war rid both Germany and Japan of an interfering, economically illiterate political leadership, and thus enabled businesspeople, assisted by aid sensibly and honestly used, to get on with the task of rebuilding their economies. Aid can help economies grow – but only if it finds fertile institutional and cultural grounds on which to do so.

A blunt instrument

Why then has aid failed Africa so spectacularly? By its very nature, aid is a blunt instrument. The only way in which spending priorities can be set is by a political process. The resulting misallocation of resources is there for all to see. What the political class in Africa wants is to claim that it is "bringing development" to its people. The slow and tediously incremental processes that are required for consistent growth are not dramatic enough, so dams – the bigger, the better – have a higher priority than classrooms or clinics. The dam, once built, has an almost metaphysical existence; it is there in all its massiveness, a physical manifestation of the ability of the political class to "deliver development". No need to worry about maintenance, or the provision of irrigation systems to improve agricultural productivity, or roads to help the peasants get their produce to market, or reliable title registries, or anything else.

This is true whether the representatives of the political class in any given case are governments or non-governmental organisations (NGOs). Nowadays in many (though not enough) African countries, it is possible to throw out governments that do not keep their promises. NGOs are a different story and have become a major obstacle to the development of responsible politics in Africa. We all know that many well-educated people these days are in a hurry to start an NGO; in Kenya, there were more than 3,000 registered NGOs in 2007.

This is an entirely rational decision. All you have to do is learn the peculiar language that NGOs use, be adept at writing reports and proposals that flatter your sponsors and damn your rivals in government or other NGOs, and learn how to drive a 4X4. NGOs create employment, though of an economically unproductive kind, for people who feel themselves too educated or morally elevated to engage in mere commerce. No need to worry about pesky and difficult things like setting up a business that makes things that customers are prepared to buy. (In 2007, Kenya's Non-Governmental Organisations Board estimated that there were about 100,000 Kenyans employed in the NGO sector in the country and that with the number of NGOs growing at 400 a year, "bogus and briefcase NGOs" had also sprung up.)

What the donors want is to avoid being accused of doing nothing. Ever since my countryman Mohammed Amin devised new and titillating ways of filming famine victims, the clamour from the Western public has been that "something must be done". Never mind that the removal of Mengistu Haile Maryiam and his murderous regime would have done more to end famine in Ethiopia than any number of self-indulgent pop songs and concerts.

The impulse to give is a generous one, but it very quickly mutates into a form of therapy. Africans are starving. The images on television are intolerable. The individual Westerner is Croesus by Ethiopian or Somali standards and is hardly likely to feel the cost of a donation. The sense of virtue that results from a relatively small donation is very agreeable. When the next crisis erupts, write another cheque. Let them know it's Christmas again. Bah, humbug.

It would be merely diverting, if not cruel and ungrateful, to mock individual donors if this attitude didn't permeate official circles as well (where it blends with cynicism). The governments of rich countries compete to give up to one per cent of their countries' gross domestic product (GDP) in the form of aid. Those who do not are pilloried. In the midst of all the claims to be more compassionate than your political opponents, few remember to ask if the aid is doing its intended job, and those who do are considered beyond the pale.

As a result, aid corrupts. Not just in the familiar sense that African politics has become a competition to control the resources of the State for the personal benefit of the political classes, leading to outrageous disparities in wealth and feeding a continuing cycle of conflict. Much more importantly, it removes responsibility for the creation of wealth from Africa's leadership to its "development partners" and enables our political class to behave irresponsibly, safe in the knowledge that a minimum level of subsistence for its people is underwritten by outsiders, and that as long as that minimum level is maintained, the political class can continue to "eat" with impunity. This is what is meant by the constant demand that foreigners should continue to pay the bills while "respecting the sovereignty" of the supplicants. All of us have mothers who taught us that this is nonsense. Pity the poor aid minister of a Western government who knows this to be true, but is constrained by political correctness from saying so.

Good governments do not need aid to act as midwives to economic growth. Singapore relied on the persuasive powers of Lee Kuan Yew to bring Texas Instruments into the country in the 1960s and thus laid the foundation of the modern, hi-tech economy Singapore has become. The aid that Singapore needed, and received, amounted to little more than a British garrison and scholarships for its brightest students. India did not need aid to develop its outsourcing and information technology industries, let alone Bollywood. Botswana is diversifying its successful economy away from diamonds and into services with nary an aid worker or consultant in sight. The distortions created by China's economy (for which every other manufacturing nation on earth is grateful) arise as a result of homegrown factors, notably the Chinese Communist Party's greed for political and economic control. (Trade between China and Africa quadrupled between 2000 and

2006 and is projected to reach $100 billion by 2010.) Think how much worse the situation would be if the Chinese had to listen to the World Bank, IMF and the rest of the aid alphabet soup. Examples of this kind can be multiplied to include pretty much all of Southeast Asia and the Far East. What is harder to find is an example of a country that has ever grown out of a dependence on aid and stood on its own feet.

If the point of aid is to stimulate economic growth, I think it's fair to say that it has failed spectacularly as far as Africa is concerned. Even Bob Geldof must know this by now. Africans are the only people on earth who have grown poorer, whose environment is more despoiled, and who are sicker and more likely to die a violent death than they were 40 years ago. But there is too much money involved, and too many careers at stake, for aid ever to be abandoned.

Towards the end of the last century, various institutions seemed to admit that aid was a lost cause. Thus we saw the birth of "structural adjustment programmes", "poverty reduction strategies" and a whole new vocabulary invented to disguise this intellectual surrender. Aid was now a combined carrot and stick for an orthodoxy that saw privatisation, reduced numbers of civil servants, democratisation and the rest of it as precursors to economic growth. It is not that these ideas are themselves wrong. It seems to me to be self-evident that a small government that concentrates on the efficient provision of a limited number of services is in itself a good thing. Where privatisation has been conducted in a clean manner, the benefits to the consumers of the service have been equally self-evident, as Kenya's national carrier, Kenya Airways, can attest.

But I think this new approach made the same mistake as its intellectual predecessor. Having spent years lavishing money on governments on the assumption that governments – even the really bad ones – were the engines of economic growth, economic fashion changed in the Western world. But no one told the recipients of aid, who suddenly found themselves facing the demands of "accountability" and "transparency" (more meaningless aid industry words).

In the past, the aid system had become something of a game. The donors would pay countries to further their ideological purposes while pretending to "fund development". The recipients would pretend to do as they were told, exaggerating their devotion to the cause while trousering as much money as possible. This was true whether the donors were Americans, Soviets, British, French or Scandinavian. Can anyone other than a Swedish true believer in creating a welfare heaven on earth have been ignorant of the stupidity with which the Tanzanian economy was run in President Julius Nyerere's time? And yet the aid money rolled in.

The new reality merely prompted a variant of the old response from our political classes. Of course everyone believed in privatisation (as long as it benefited them or their friends); of course everyone believed in a small, efficient government (as long as their tribesmen were not fired); of course everyone believed in transparency and accountability (except in matters of "national strategic interest", such as, well everything, really).

And so the game continued. Various leaders, such as Kenya's former President Daniel arap Moi, became masters of manipulation. He pretended to obey, but in fact spent all of his time subverting reforms that he knew would finish off his regime if they were implemented. Various IMF and World Bank country heads cajoled, threatened, wrote and said rude things, stormed out of meetings etc. But they always came back and continued their little game as Moi knew they would, if only because they had to justify their own existence (not to mention their very pleasant jobs and lifestyles).

The failure of aid to achieve anything concrete leads to its constant reinvention, in the desperate hope that fervour and persistence will eventually turn this sow's ear into a silk purse. This is the other important sense in which aid corrupts. It means that the dialogue between Africa and the world is fundamentally dishonest, because it is clear that aid will do nothing to improve the standard of living of all but an infinitesimal minority of Africans. If the point of it is something else – perhaps aid is a polite way to enforce reparations for the exploitation or underdevelopment of Africa? – then I think we should come clean and admit it, and tell the donors to find something else to keep their consciences warm. But if we are serious about growth in Africa, we need to take off the aid diaper and learn to make our own way like all the other grown-ups in this world.

13

THE MAKING OF AN AFRICAN NGO

Issa G. Shivji

Recently, African poverty has moved to the centrestage of the development world, thanks to the likes of leaders such as Tony Blair. Non-governmental organisations (NGOs) in Africa echo and repeat the slogan generated by their Northern benefactors: "Make Poverty History".

But how can you make poverty history without understanding the history of poverty? We need to know how the poverty of the so-called developing world came about just as we need to know even more accurately how the filthy riches of the biggest multinationals and wealthiest people were created. We need to know even more precisely how this great divide, this unbridgeable chasm, is maintained, reproduced and increasingly deepened and widened. We need to ask ourselves: What are the political, social, moral, ideological, economic and cultural mechanisms that produce and reinforce, and make such a world not only possible, but acceptable?

Unfortunately, the NGO discourse seems to have internalised the thoughtless idiocies of right-wing reactionary writers who propagate the "end of history" in which the present – that is, of course, the global capitalism under the hegemony of the imperialist North – is declared *permanent*. Any historical understanding of our present condition is ridiculed and dismissed, or tolerated as a token to create the illusion of "diversity". In the African setting, any discussion of colonial history invariably elicits the standard response: Let us stop blaming the colonialists! How long shall we continue lamenting about colonialism? Thus history is reduced to, and then ridiculed as a "blaming exercise".

And yet colonial and imperial history is at the heart of the present African condition. History is not about assigning or sharing blame, nor is it about narrating a "past" that must be forgotten and forgiven or only remembered once a year on Heroes Remembrance Day or Independence Day. History is about the *present*. We must understand the *present as history* so as to change it for the better. This is especially urgent in the African context, where the imperial project is not only historical, it is the present. Just as we cannot "make poverty history" without understanding the history of poverty, so we cannot chant "another world is possible" without accurately understanding and correctly describing the existing world of five billion slaves and 200 slave masters.

"SAP-ping" the African state to death

Colonialism left through the front door and returned through the back door in the form of what Kwame Nkrumah called neo-colonialism. In Africa, the armed struggles in Mozambique, Angola and Guinea Bissau represented, ironically, both the high point of radical nationalism and its precipitous decline in the next decade. And in South Africa, the "success" of one of the longest and most militant national liberation movements was not so much the high point of the struggle of radical nationalism against imperialism, but rather the beginning of its end.

On the heels of the defeat of the national project came the imperialist offensive to destroy and bury it. On the economic front, the neoliberal package boiled down to further deepening the integration of African economies into the world capitalist system, thus reproducing the colonial and neo-colonial economic structures.

In 1981, the World Bank published its notorious report *Accelerated Development for Africa: An Agenda for Africa*. It was certainly an agenda for Africa set by the Bretton Woods institutions with the backing of Western countries, but it had little to do with development, accelerated or otherwise. The report and the subsequent structural adjustment programmes (SAPs) concentrated on stabilisation measures: getting rid of budget deficits, bringing down rates of inflation, getting prices right, unleashing the market and liberalising trade. According to the World Bank, the villain of the declining economic performance in Africa was the state; it was corrupt and dictatorial, it had no capacity to manage the economy and allocate resources rationally, it was bloated with bureaucracy, and nepotism was its mode of operation. The Bretton Woods institutions would thus not bail out Africa's crisis-ridden economies unless the governments adopted SAPs to get stabilisation fundamentals right.

Balancing budgets involved cutting subsidies to agriculture and social programmes, including health and education. Unleashing the market meant doing away with protection of infant industries and rolling back the state from economic activity. The results were devastating. Social indicators, such as education, medical care, health, nutrition, rates of literacy and life expectancy, all declined. Deindustrialisation set in. Redundancies followed. In short, even the modest achievements of the nationalist or developmentalist period were lost or undermined.

As the international situation was turned upside down by the collapse of the Soviet Union, Western imperialist powers regained their ideological initiative. The neo-liberal package of marketisation, privatisation and liberalisation now became the policy *for*, but not *of* the African State. Good performers would be praised and rewarded with more aid while the insubordinate and the recalcitrant would be parodied and left to their own devices. While aid had always come with strings attached, now there was no attempt to disguise it. Political conditionalities – multipartyism, good governance, human rights etc. – were added to economic conditionalities. Political decision-making and policy-making slipped out of the hands of the African State as Western-financed policy, finance and governance consultants in their thousands jetted all over the continent with blue prints of policies on Poverty Reduction Strategies and manuals on good governance on their computers, gobbling up some $4 billion annually.[1]

African leaders were left with just two options: To join the neo-liberal globalisation bandwagon or be doomed.

They fell into line one after another even if it meant disowning their own past. The Tony Blair-led Commission for Africa, which consisted of prominent Africans, including one president and one prime minister, castigated the whole of the past three decades – virtually the whole post-independence period – as "lost decades". The primary responsibility was placed on the African State for bad governance and lack of accountability, totally ignoring the role of imperialism in both the exploitation of African resources and support of non-democratic states when it suited their interests. African countries were told they had no capacity to make correct policies. Blair's Commission for Africa declared with a straight face:

> "Africa's history over the last fifty years has been blighted by two areas of weakness. These have been *capacity* – the ability to design and deliver policies; and *accountability* – how well a state answers to its people."[2]

So policy-making, an important aspect of sovereignty, was wrenched out of the hands of the African state. In policy-making, the state was placed on the same level as other so-called stakeholders, the NGOs.

Meanwhile, the African people, who were once the authors and drivers of development and liberators of their nations, were reduced to "the chronically poor" who were the subjects of papers on strategies for poverty reduction authored by consultants and discussed at stakeholders workshops in which "the poor" were represented by NGOs. The poor, the diseased, the disabled, the Aids-infected, the ignorant, the marginalised, in short the "people", were not part of the development equation, since development was assigned to private capital that constituted the "engine of growth". "The poor" were just recipients of humanitarian aid; they neither produced nor created wealth.

In current neo-liberal discourse, the African state is villainised and African bureaucracies are demonised as corrupt, incapable and unable to learn. African countries are therefore seen as in need of globalised foreign advisors and consultants – who are now referred to as development practitioners – to mentor, monitor and oversee them. Among the mentors and monitors are, of course, NGOs. After all, the so-called advisors and consultants move freely between the "Triad Family" – the DONs (donor organisations), the INFOs (international financial organisations) and the NGOs, including the GoNGOs (government-organised NGOs) and DoNGOs (donor-organised NGOs).

In this discourse, the developmental role of the state is declared dead and buried. Instead, it is assigned the role of "chief" to supervise the globalisation project under the tutelage of imperialism. The irony of the Commission for Africa was that it was convened, constituted and chaired by a British prime minister, while an African president and an African prime minister sat on it as members. This symbolises the nature of the "new partnership". The message is clear: African "co-partners" in African development are neither equal nor in the driver's seat.

It is true that the neo-liberal discourse has not gone without being challenged, both intellectually and practically. African people have fought on the streets against SAPs; they have protested in their own ways in their villages and towns and neighbourhoods. African intellectuals have written and argued and shown the fallacy of the underlying assumptions of neo-liberalism and globalisation. Nevertheless, at least for the time being, neo-liberalism seems to hold sway. Virtually the whole of the African political elite and establishment (unlike, for example, in Latin America) has fallen into line, whether for pragmatic reasons of survival or to defend their own vested interests. A large part of the African intellectual elite too have been co-opted and accommodated within the neo-colonial discourse.

The five silences in the NGO discourse
The rapid rise of NGOs and their apparently prominent role in Africa is part of the neo-liberal organisational, and particularly ideological, offensive. At the inception of the neo-liberal offensive in the early 1980s, the rise and role of

NGOs was explained and justified within the conceptual framework of the problematic of civil society. (The concept of civil society came into vogue in the 1980s with the impending collapse of the Soviet and Eastern European systems and the democratisation drive in Africa.) Influenced heavily, as always, by US-based Africanists, it is the false bi-polarity or dichotomy between the state and civil society that has predominated. Within neo-liberal ideologies, the state is demonised and civil society, often conflated with NGOs, is celebrated. Non-governmental organisations are presented as the "third sector", the other two being the state (power, politics) and the private sector (capital, economics). This ideological presentation of non-government organisation is also the dominant self-perception of the NGO world. Yet it is based on utterly false historical and intellectual premises, with serious political implications.

Here I describe what I refer to as "the five silences in the NGO discourse" that show that NGOs are inextricably embedded in the neoliberal offensive that followed on the heels of the national project crisis.

First, a large number of African NGOs were born in the womb of the neo-liberal offensive that began to open up some space for freedom of association. One of the features of the statist period was the organisational hegemony of the state. In the first flush of the opening up of organisation space, NGOs proliferated without critical examination of the place and role of the NGO and its underlying ideologies and premises. The anti-state stance of the so-called donor community was the real push behind the upsurge in NGO activity.

Second, African NGOs are led by, and largely composed of, the educated elite, located in urban areas and well-versed in the language and idiom of modernisation. Broadly, three types of NGO elite may be identified. First is the radical elite that was previously involved in political struggles with an explicit vision of change and transformation but that found itself suppressed under the threat of statist hegemony. Many of these elites took the opportunity to express themselves politically in the NGOs. They saw NGOs as a possible terrain of struggle for change. This section of the elite is essentially politically motivated without being necessarily involved in partisan party politics. The second category includes well-intentioned individuals driven by altruistic motives to better the conditions of their fellow human beings/compatriots. In other words, they are morally motivated. Third are the mainstream elite, not infrequently even former government bureaucrats, who shifted to the NGO world once they found that that was where the donor funding was directed. The motivation of this elite is quite simply careerist. It is driven by material gains rather than altruistic motives. It is personally motivated. This category keeps swelling as jobs within government and in the private sector become more and more competitive or difficult to come by.

Third, an overwhelming number of African NGOs are donor-funded. They do not have any independent source of funding and have to seek donor funds through the usual procedures set up by the funding agencies. In this respect, the degree of independence they can exert in relation to donor agendas varies from NGO to NGO, depending on the perspectives of its leadership. In practice, though, as would be readily acknowledged by even the most radical among them, their scope of action is limited. This does not necessarily mean that a few may not exercise greater autonomy in their outlook and ideology and be still accepted; exceptions are necessary to prove the rule.

While some NGOs may be quite involved with and appreciated by the people who they purport to serve, ultimately NGOs, by their very nature, derive not only their sustenance but also their legitimacy from the donor community. In the current international conjuncture, even political elites located in the state or political parties seek legitimacy from the so-called development partners, rather than from their own people. Not surprisingly, there is a fair amount of circulation of the elite between the government and the non-government sectors.

Fourth, a significant number of African NGOs are

advocacy NGOs, focusing on particular areas of activity, such as human rights, gender, Aids, environment and governance. While there are always NGOs set up by politically or morally motivated individuals with a genuine desire to "do something", and which genuinely mean to respond to the needs of the people, it is also true that a substantial number of NGOs are set up to respond to what is perceived to be in vogue among the donor community at any particular time. Donor-driven NGOs, I would guess, are the most dominant.

Besides advocacy tasks, NGOs are also increasingly commissioned by donors, or the state, or even the corporate sector, to do consultancy work for them or to be their executive agencies to dispense funds or services. Thus NGOs have come to play a major role in the "aid and development industry". In the NGO world, it is not at all ironical that a non-governmental body is assigned by the government to do a governmental job funded by a donor agency that is itself an outfit of a foreign government. Thus the US Agency for International Development (USAID) may fund a gender NGO to raise awareness among women on the new land law whose terms of reference are set by a government ministry. To complete the picture, one may find that the same USAID has recommended and sponsored a consultant who drafted the land law for the government in the first place. This completes the "holy trinity" of development partners: the state, capital and NGOs.

Fifth, while most African NGOs may insert visions or mission statements (such as "empowerment" or "poverty-reduction") in their charters, these are vague, amorphous and often meaningless. In any case, they are quickly forgotten and what takes over are the so-called strategic plans and "log frames" that can be tabulated, quantified and ticked for reports and proposals for more funding. The "success" of an NGO is measured by how efficiently it is managed and run and the criteria for measuring efficiency are borrowed from the corporate sector. Training NGOs are set up to train NGO managers in "strategic framework analysis", in charting "inputs" and "outcomes", in setting indicators and in methods and techniques to log the vision and the mission and the strategy in log frames.

Thus, just as the colonial enterprise assumed the garb of a civilising mission and used the church as its *avant-garde*, so the globalisation pundits don the clothing of secular human rights and use NGOs as their ideological foot soldiers.

The international and national orders within which we are functioning are unequal and have conflicting interests. To pretend that society is a harmonious whole of stakeholders is to be complicit in perpetuating the status quo in the interest of the dominant classes and powers. In the struggle between national liberation and imperialist domination and between social emancipation and capitalist slavery, NGOs have to choose sides. There are no in-betweens.

If African NGOs are to play the role of catalysts of change rather than catechists of aid and charity, they have to fundamentally re-examine their silences and their discourses; they must scrutinise the philosophical and political premises that underpin their activities; they must investigate the credentials of their development partners and the motives of their financial benefactors; they must distance themselves from oppressive African states and compradorial ruling elites. NGOs must refuse to legitimise, rationalise and provide a veneer of respectability and morality to global pillage by voracious transnationals under the guise of creating a global village.

I dare say that if in the NGO world we understood well the history of poverty and enslavement in Africa, if we scrutinised the credentials of the so-called development partners, if we distanced ourselves from the oppressive African state, if we refused to lend our names to "poverty reduction policies and strategies" that are meant to legitimise the rich, if indeed, we vowed to be catalysts of change and refused to be catechists of charity, we would be toyi-toyi-ing at the doorsteps of Blair and his commissioners, beating our tom-toms and singing "Make Imperialism History" instead of jumping on the bandwagon of Sir Bob Geldof's Band Aid.

Notes

[1] Mwandawire, T. and Soludo, C.C. (Eds.). 1999. *Our Continent, Our Future: African Perspectives on Structural Adjustment*, Dakar: CODESRIA.

[2] Commission for Africa, "Our Common Interest: Report of the Commission for Africa", March 2005, p.12

14

THE DEPOLITICISATION OF POVERTY

Firoze Manji

Reflecting on the achievements of the last 50 years, some might be forgiven for feeling that African countries have little to celebrate. The social gains of independence from colonial rule in the 1960s have been rapidly eroded as African economies collapsed under the combined weight of debt and structural adjustment programmes in the 1990s.

Every year, the United Nations calculates the human development index (HDI) based on a series of measures including the prevalence of illiteracy, life expectancy, degree of malnourishment, and access to health services and safe water. Over the last decade, the HDI has been rising in almost all countries except those in sub-Saharan Africa. Twelve of the 18 countries that registered lower scores on the HDI in 2003 than in 1990 are in sub-Saharan Africa. This means some 240 million people on the continent are worse off today than they were 15 years ago.[1] Levels of poverty on the continent are increasing in the context of a number of conflicts, both in Africa, and in other parts of the world. The UN admits that while the number of conflicts around the world have fallen since 1990, they are becoming more bloody and protracted. In 2005, The UNDP's *Human Development Report* noted:

> Since 1990 the world has witnessed genocide in Rwanda, violent civil wars in the heart of Europe, wars in Afghanistan and Iraq and setbacks in the Middle East. The conflict in the Democratic Republic of the Congo has claimed almost 4 million lives – the greatest death toll since the Second World War. In Sudan a peace settlement in the one of Africa's

longest running civil wars served as a prelude to a new humanitarian crisis in Darfur, with more than 1 million people displaced.[2]

Such conflicts are frequently portrayed as being the result of apparent "irreconcilable ethnic differences" that not only pervade the continent today, but are also viewed as intrinsic to the history of the continent. Mass human rights violations are seen, therefore, as an "inevitable", if regrettable, consequence of these "ethnic" conflicts.

Growing impoverishment, conflict and the increasing number of apparently ethnic-based conflicts have a common origin. They are the products of a process that began as popular mobilisation against oppression and exploitation — a movement for rights — that ultimately became warped into a process that became known as "development ". Far from helping to overturn the social relations that reproduced injustice and impoverishment, the main focus of development was to discover and implement solutions that would enable the victims to cope with, or find "sustainable" solutions for living with, impoverishment. Over the last few decades development NGOs have played a critical role in that process. Their roles have gradually changed from an embryonic anti-imperialism to becoming an integral part of postcolonial social formations.

Africa is a lens that discloses the general characteristics of development. The features are not particular to the continent; they are to be found also in Asia and Latin America, albeit tinted by the specific histories of those regions. By focusing on Africa, the complex inter-relationships between rights, poverty and development can be revealed with the knowledge that those in Asia and Latin America will find the resonance of sounds that speak to their own experience.

The model of development itself is the cause of some of the major conflicts that have arisen in the region, including those that led to the genocide in Central Africa. The role of NGOs in the depoliticisation of poverty is examined in the context of these developments.

From rights to "development"

The story of independence in Africa is frequently portrayed as the story of the machinations of nationalist leaders in mobilising popular agitations against the colonial powers and their prowess at the negotiation tables. What is frequently omitted in that account is the story of what was happening on the ground, in the forests, villages, urban ghettos, classrooms and in workplaces, in spite of – not because of — the nationalist leaders.

The initial spark for most people was provided by the desire to organise around the right to food, shelter, water, land, education and health care; around the right to freedom of association, freedom of speech, freedom of movement, freedom from harassment and other forms of human rights abuses. Different groups within society organised around issues with which they were themselves most preoccupied — aspiring local capitalists organising around restraints on their freedom to accumulate, while squatters organised around their rights of access to land.

These struggles laid the basis in many countries for the emergence of a national consciousness that would provide some legitimacy to the nation state that was about to be established. But that dynamic was not to be permitted to reach its logical conclusion. While the liberation struggles had begun the process of forging a common national identity, this identity remained fragile at the time of hand-over of power, even in those countries (such as Mozambique, Angola and Guinea Bissau) which had to undergo protracted wars of liberation.

Once thrown into power, the nationalist leadership (comprising mainly representatives of the newly emerging middle class) saw its task as one of preventing "centrifugal forces" from competing for political power or seeking greater autonomy from the newly formed "nation". Having grasped political self-determination from colonial authority, it was reluctant to accord the same rights to others. The new occupiers of the state machinery saw their role as the "sole developer" and "sole unifier" of society. The state defined for itself an interventionist role in "modernisation" and a centralising and controlling role in the political realm.

Born out of a struggle for the legitimacy of pluralism against a hegemonic colonial state, social pluralism began to be frowned upon. The popular associations that had thrown the nationalist leadership into power gradually began to be seen as an obstacle to the new god of "development". No longer was there a need, it was argued, for popular participation in determining the future. The new governments would bring development to the people. The new government, they claimed, represented the nation and everyone in it. Now that political independence had been achieved, the priority was "development". Social and economic improvements would come with patience and as a result of combined national effort involving all classes ["harambee" (pulling together), in Jomo Kenyatta's famous slogan]. In this early period after independence, civil and political rights soon came to be seen as a "luxury", to be enjoyed at some unspecified time in the future when "development" had been achieved. For the present, said many African presidents, "our people are not ready" - mirroring, ironically, the same arguments used by the former colonial rulers against the nationalists' cries for independence a few years earlier.

In the colonial era, government social services for Africans were almost nonexistent. Where they were provided, the purpose was largely to ensure the integrity of the structures of colonial rule. In periods of serious outbreaks of epidemics in the shantytowns and overcrowded ghettos, health services were provided principally to stave off the possibilities of infections spreading into white society. In some instances, limited education was provided when certain basic skills would be necessary for the administration of the colony or for the particular forms of exploitation. For the vast majority of the rural population, it was left to a clutch of charities and missionary groups (what in today's jargon would be recognised as NGOs) to exchange their spiritual wares for material support in education, health or other social services. For white settlers or the agents of colonial rule, however, state expenditure on the social sector was usually generous. Although on the eve of independence there were to be significant changes in the extent to which investments were to be made in the social sectors, for the most part the state's function in these sectors was to provide only for a minority.

The situation was to change dramatically at independence. It remains one of the most remarkable, and yet least acknowledged, achievements of independence governments that within the space of but a few years, access to health services and to education was to become effectively universal. No matter how much one may criticise the forms of services provided, it is a tribute to the capacity of the state to implement such far-reaching social programmes. While NGOs may today debate and shower praises on each other about their own capacities to "scale up", the new governments at independence implemented programmes of "scaling-up" in a manner that no NGO has ever dared to imagine. The impact of these interventions are undeniable and were to be reflected in the subsequent dramatic changes in average life expectancy, in infant and child mortality rates, and in the improvements in nutritional status of the young. Huge improvements in all these parameters were to be observed throughout the continent by the end of the 1970s as a result of these social programmes. Aggregate figures for sub-Saharan Africa show, for example, that life expectancy increased from 38 years in 1960 to 47 years in 1978, despite the fact that GNP per capita increased only modestly from $222 to $280[3].

But at the same time as this infrastructure was being built (often with the financial support of official aid agencies), a transformation had taken place which led to a demobilisation of the popular movement that had given rise to independence. Popular organisations that had emerged out of the struggle for rights (social, political, economic or civil) were provided no further role in the process. Rights were no longer the flag around which the oppressed could rally. Indeed, the concept of rights was codified and rarefied in laws and constitutions whose relevance or application was determined by the self-proclaimed, and increasingly unaccountable, guardians of the state. A gradual shift took place where concerns about rights and justice were replaced by concerns about "development". Certainly there were major problems faced by the newly independent states in addressing how the forces of production (whether industrial or agricultural) could be developed to drag Africa out of the destitution created by colonial rule. But the discourse was not about development in the sense of developing the productive forces. It was about creating an infrastructure that advanced the capacity of the new ruling class to accumulate and smoothing those inefficiencies that hampered the capacity of international capital to continue its exploitation of the country. It was expected that, through trickle-down effects, poverty would gradually be eliminated. This was the agenda of "modernisation", the paradigm of development that was to hold sway until the end of the 1970s.

The age of the development expert
Central to this paradigm was to cast "poverty", rather than social justice, as the main problem facing "developing countries". The victims of years of injustices, whose livelihoods had been destroyed by years of colonial rule, were now defined as "the problem", and once so defined provided the stage set for the entry of the development NGO to participate in the process of depoliticising poverty. In Kenya, for example, peasants had been uprooted from their land and forced to eke out a living in marginal land with low yield potential and which required immense labour to produce. The new paradigm required that ways be found to enable them to find sustainable (and participatory) approaches for surviving on such land. The need for carrying out land reform that would overcome the injustices created by colonialism was gradually forgotten.

The structures of accountability and democracy that were inherent in the movements centred on rights were gradually marginalised and replaced by the ascendancy of the expert supported by bureaucratic and centralised decision making under the guise of "national planning". Political associations were soon to be discouraged, if not actually banned, while trade unions were constrained, incorporated into the structures of the ruling party, or simply disbanded. In many countries those structures that had emerged to organise around basic rights had all been either subsumed under "development" or discarded within ten years of independence. The political hegemony of the new post-independence rulers had been asserted. Their capacity to attend to the "basic needs" of the population gave them some legitimacy and allowed, in some instances, reasonable national cohesion. But the development of national consciousness, born fragile and imperfectly in the struggle for rights in the 1950s and 1960s, began to lose sustenance, its life-blood dissipating. The age of the development expert, the relief expert, and subsequently the conflict resolution expert, had arrived.

The "misuse" of the state was to become a critical factor in the distortions brought to the development agenda. Patronage was used frequently to buy favours with different groups in the country. The purpose of development programmes was distorted to ensure progress was brought not to where there was the greatest social or economic need. Instead it was brought to where investment would serve the need to curry favour with particular social or "ethnic" groups whose political alliance was deemed useful at a particular time and where the possibilities for private accumulation by the elite were greatest. Under such conditions, it was hardly surprising that competition for access to resources increasingly manifested themselves along "ethnic" lines. With the demise or suppression of organizations based on the struggle for rights, old social alliances based on perceived historical grievances against other "ethnic" groups re-emerged. The seeds of subsequent conflicts were already taking root.

Structural adjustment and the rise of conflicts

The economic crisis that emerged out of the "oil crisis" in the 1970s was characterised by a huge glut of capital. Europe and America were suddenly awash with capital with few opportunities for high rates of return. Although many African countries already had heavy debts, there is little doubt that the surfeit of capital created by the oil crisis provided a qualitative encouragement to increase the debt burden. As a result, developing countries were courted to take loans to finance "development". Although the absolute size of debt of sub-Saharan African countries was relatively small in proportion to the external indebtedness of developing countries, the size of the debt (and the cost of servicing that debt) in relation to the resources and productive capacity of these African countries were significantly large.

But that glut was short-lived. Coinciding with the period of the emerging technological revolution in microcomputers and in gene technology that attracted capital to new fields where the rates of profit were likely to be substantial, the 1980s saw significant increases in the cost of borrowing. As interest rates rose, and debtor countries were suddenly faced with servicing the interest on loans that absorbed the ever-greater proportions of export earnings. Debt had now the central issue of "concern" in development circles.

The Bretton Woods institutions that, in the post-war period, had invested so heavily to ensure the resuscitation of economies of Europe, became the new commanders of third world economies. A clutch of social and economic policies that came to be known as structural adjustment programmes (SAPs) were applied, in the spirit of universality, across the board. The social and political impact of these policies was to position the multilateral lending agencies (with the support of the bilateral aid agencies) where they could determine both the goals of development and the means for achieving them. It legitimised their direct intervention in political decision-making processes, enabling them, for example, to set the levels of producer and consumer prices. These institutions literally determined the extent of involvement that the state should have in the social sector, and insisted on the state imposing draconian economic and social measures that resulted in a rise in unemployment and the decline in real incomes of the majority. The result was to transform and restructure the social basis of power in African countries, strengthening those forces or alliances that would be sympathetic to the continued hegemony of the multilaterals and of the multinationals.

These measures had the effect of exacerbating the divisions between the "haves" and the "have-nots", between those who, for political or for reasons of patronage, received benefits and those who did not. And the old, discredited theories of "trickledown" now ardently promoted by the IMF and World Bank, were embraced as the only legitimate way of enjoying the fruits of independence. Popular dissatisfaction with the policies of the government led in the 1980s to spontaneous demonstrations, burning of crops, wildcat strikes, and similar expressions of discontent. Universities were closed, demonstrations brutally suppressed, strikes declared illegal. Trade unions, student organisations, popular movements, and political parties became the target of repressive legislation or actions.

Such widespread opposition resulted in some rethinking by official aid agencies and the multilaterals about how to present the same economic and social programmes with a more "human face". Significant volumes of funds were set aside aimed at "mitigating" the "social dimensions of adjustment". The aim of such programmes was to act as palliatives that might minimise the more glaring inequalities that their policies had perpetuated. Funds were made available to ensure that social services for the "vulnerable" would be provided - but this time not by the state (which had after all been forced to "retrench" away from the social sector) but by the ever willing NGO sector. The availability of such funds for the NGO sector was to have a profound impact on the very nature of that sector.

"When elephants fight the grass gets trampled"

The material basis for the rise of conflicts in Africa had therefore been laid. A popular movement that had once organised itself around the struggle for rights and justice had been demobilised either through repression or by redirecting its attention to the apparently neutral territory of "development". The process of democratisation of the colonial state had been limited to deracialisation of urban civil society, while the rural peasantry remained constricted within the structures of Native Authority established under colonialism. The development process itself had become as source of accumulation and patronage. Structural adjustment programmes exacerbated social differentiation. As the pie got smaller with the debt crisis and the deteriorating terms of trade, so the state became more repressive. And just as had happened in the 1920s in another era, in the rural areas numerous religious and quasi-religious organisations, sects and other such movements emerged as the source of social solidarity, some entirely based on ethnic membership, others more diverse. And in the urban centres, the only tolerated form of organisation became the network of criminal organisations that rooted themselves in the periurban ghettos of Africa's cities.

With the collapse of the Berlin Wall, the credibility of movements offering an alternative ideology to the Thatcherite "get-rich-quick-beggar-thy-neighbour" capitalism also collapsed. Opposition was no longer a function of alternative ideas or policies or about of who could enhance development, but now an open and frank fight in the market place for economic hegemony. The collapse of ideology led thus to the legitimisation of ruthless competition, competition that was, in the absence of legitimate mechanisms for constraint or credible state machinery able to mediate the competition, increasingly conducted by the most ruthless means, and in some cases (e.g. Sierra Leone, Liberia) using military means. The distinction between social organisation for criminal activities and for political purposes became blurred. Civilians became increasingly caught in the crossfire or as the targets either of armed opposition groups or of the increasingly desperate state machinery. Arrest and imprisonment of political opponents, once a critical focus for international protest against the despotic state, had now become a less frequently used form of repression. Instead, disappearances, political killings and extrajudicial executions were the order of the day

If the development process has become about who gets

access to what, then civil war is but a continuation of that process by other, albeit more destructive, means. Civil war has frequently become the inexorable outcome of the development process itself. In Sierra Leone both the army and the "rebels" were the main actors in the mining industry. The war in Liberia became a lucrative venture for illegal mining, drug trafficking and money laundering. Angola's protracted war helped Jonas Savimbi and some multinational corporations to extract diamonds from the country: in 1993 alone, Savimbi's rebel group pocketed $250 million from the mining towns that it controlled. The South African mining conglomerate De Beers has admitted to buying illegally diamonds mined in Angola worth some $500 million. In 1992 alone, money laundered from drugs in war-torn countries amounted to about $856 million.

The conflict which took place in Rwanda in 1994 was a human catastrophe of immense proportions. But its underlying causes are a tragic example of the consequences of the combination of the factors that have been referred to above. The collapse of the International Coffee Agreement had a devastating effect on more than 70% of households in the country, and Rwandan farmers expressed their anger and frustration in 1992 by cutting down some 3,000 coffee trees. This exacerbated the tensions that had been fuelled by the attempted invasion of the Rwandese Patriotic Front (RPF). The government read the political mood and understood that its legitimacy was being challenged. In desperation it became more repressive, disseminating hate propaganda against the supposed "enemy", the Tutsi, and encouraging systematic killings and violations against any who they defined as being Tutsi or the allies of Tutsi. The defence component of the government's already over-stretched budget increased substantially, the size of the army being increased from a mere 5,000 to over 40,000 soldiers. That was the context in which the World Bank insisted on the implementation of its standard package of social and economic policies of reducing public expenditure, privatisation, retrenchment, and making people pay more for health and education. The effect was to increase the burden on the majority of Rwandese, 85% of whom were living below the poverty line. In the context of the disintegration of fragile political institutions, the political impasse within the government itself over the Arusha Accords that proposed power sharing with the RPF, anything could have triggered off the conflict. And that indeed happened when the presidential plane was shot down in April 1994.

The role of NGOs in depoliticising poverty

What, then, has been the role of the non-governmental development agencies in this turbulent history?

Development NGOs will vehemently claim that their work in developing countries is neutral. This assumption of neutrality probably has its origins in the heroic work that NGOs have frequently performed in response to crises. Under such circumstances, NGOs have adopted the essential humanitarian principle that all those affected by disasters should be treated equally and receive assistance equally. Humanitarian responses should take no sides in conflicts. The problem arises when these same principles have been applied in non-crisis conditions such as those that prevail in "development" programmes or, in conditions of prolonged crises especially where, for example as in Somalia, the state itself has long ago collapsed.

But is there a space wherein NGOs can carry out their charitable work without "taking sides" in the process of reproduction of these social relations? I believe not. The fact is that many NGOs have, unwittingly or willingly, inserted themselves over the last few decades as part of the very infrastructure of the political economy that reproduces the unequal social relations of post-colonial Africa.

That has not always been the case. In the period of anti-colonial struggles, many NGOs actively participated in solidarity movements or in supporting directly anti-imperialist organisations. Their participation in such activities was informed by their (albeit intuitive) understanding that existing social relations of colonial rule needed to be overthrown. The same was also true of those NGOs who participated in the antiapartheid movement or supported the work of the Mass Democratic Movement in South Africa prior to the release of Nelson Mandela.

But with independence, the dilemma that NGOs faced (and one that many have faced in South Africa recently) was a difficult one: the *ancien regime* had been overthrown. The conditions for its reproduction had been destroyed. Surely the role of NGOs should now be to participate in the process of ensuring the reproduction of the new regime, the new social order? And surely, the answer to that should be in the affirmative? But only, I believe, in so far as the new social order was not intent on the perpetuation of old or the creation new injustices or forms of exploitation.

But how were NGOs to know how things would turn out in the future?

Caught in the torrent of upheavals that characterised the victory over colonialism (and against apartheid), it was easy to become romantic and blinkered by one's own enthusiasm. It was hardly surprising that many NGOs became closely involved in "bringing development to the people" in the newly independent countries. But the real problem was that the dominant discourse on development was framed not in the language of rights and justice, but with the vocabulary of charity, technical expertise, neutrality, and a deep paternalism (albeit accompanied by the rhetoric of participatory development) which was its syntax.

This was a period in which the involvement of Northern NGOs in Africa grew dramatically. The number of international NGOs operating in Kenya, for example, increased almost three-fold to 134 organisations during the period 1978 to 1988[4]. Most of the northern NGOs preoccupied themselves with "projects" that would benefit "the poor" and whose main purpose was to bring "development" to the people. As repression of those who were seen to be political opponents became a feature of the new state centralising its control, many NGOs chose to remain silent about creeping repression. Protest against repression of political opponents was largely left to (northern) human rights organisations. The dilemma faced by NGOs was that such protests could jeopardise the grants that they received from the official aid agencies (who, certainly until the mid 1980s, rarely sought to comment on the excesses of African governments). NGOs, especially the Northern ones, also feared that protest could jeopardise their own relationship with the national government to whom they were beholden for a range of privileges (tax or duty exemptions etc.). There was little point, some argued, in making a fuss since "it would only be the poor who would suffer as a result".

Over time, their role evolved from their anti-colonial past to becoming one of the central actors in the process of development itself. NGOs, especially those from the North, began to insert themselves as vital cogs in the new political economy, the vehicles through which an increasing proportion of development programmes were implemented. They were armed with manuals and all the technical know-how for focusing the attention of "the poor" on coping with the present rather than seeking justice for past crimes against them. Like their missionary predecessors, they offered the poor blessings in the future (albeit on earth rather than in heaven). And as aid budgets in the North declined, and as greater volumes of funds were made available through direct funding, so Northern NGOs sought to accommodate to the new environment by legally registering themselves as "local NGOs" the better to tap the vast sums available locally. One of the effects of the latter has been to transform the Northern NGO from being a donor/supporter of local NGOs, to becoming a direct competitor for aid funds in the local market. In the meantime, hundreds of local NGOs were established whose sole purpose was to become the subcontractors for the provision of social services that would mitigate the effects of adjustment for the "vulnerable" or "poorest of the poor".

And in the process, concerns about the rights of the vast majority of the population, their search for freedom from oppression and exploitation, had become peripheral. Northern NGOs in particular were now more preoccupied with fundraising on the basis of portraying Africans as the subject of pity and whose plight would be relieved through acts of charity. In the region, this approach served to demobilisation and disillusion. In the North, the public's prejudices were reinforced about Africans as hopeless, as mere victims of endless civil war, and as passive recipients of Northern charity.

But was it inevitable that NGOs would become so thoroughly integrated in to the political economy of Africa as to become partners in the reproduction of social relations that give rise to impoverishment and conflict? Is it inevitable that they will continue to do so?

The cynical view is perhaps that the development NGO has long ago developed a vested interest in the continued reproduction of such social relations, and that they will "do better the less stable the world becomes ... [because] ... finance will become increasingly available to agencies who can deliver 'stabilising' social services."[5]

I believe that the option exists for NGOs to chose otherwise if they recognise that there is no "neutral" ground, no "no-man's land" in the process of development. Those who believe there is neutral territory frequently become prey to the agendas of other social forces. They would do well to reflect on the following excerpt from a USAID review that was quoted by Nelson Mandela in his recent report to the ANC Congress:

Two-thirds of [US]AID's funding ... is used to fund AID-dependent NGOs ... The Old 'struggle NGOs' have been redesignated by AID as 'civil service organisations' (or CSOs). AID now funds CSOs to 'monitor public policy, provide information, and advocate policy alternatives' and to serve as 'sentinels, brokers and arbiters for the public will.' The purpose of AID's funding is to enable these CSOs to 'function as effective policy advocacy groups' and 'to lobby'... Through its NGOs, AID intends to play a key role in domestic policy concerning the most difficult, controversial issues of national politics. AID's political agenda is ambitious and extensive.[6]

The choice is thus a stark one: either play the role (unwittingly or otherwise) of reinforcing those social relations that reproduce impoverishment, injustice and conflict. Or, make the choice to play a positive role in supporting those processes in society that will overturn those social relations.

The alternative is to stand impotent and bewildered as NGOs did when the genocide erupted in Rwanda. Impotent because they did not understand what could have been done, and bewildered because of an unease that the processes of development in Africa, of which NGOs have become such an integral part, themselves gave rise to the conflicts and to the terrors of genocide.

The slogan that gave rise to the Universal Declaration of Human Rights was "never again" to genocide. There is a bitter irony in the fact that when it happened again in Africa, the signatories to that proclamation were silent or unwilling to act. Rwanda has demonstrated that the proclamation was deficient. It remains for popular movements and organisations of Africa to rebuild the tradition based on its own experiences that can guarantee the conditions in which genocide will never again be possible.

That will be no easy task. Whether or not development NGOs can participate in that process will depend largely on whether they continue to define their role as part of the political economy of a form of development that breeds and sustains inequalities and conflicts, or whether they rally to the standard of solidarity and rights. The choice is theirs.

Notes

[1] UN Development Programme (UNDP). 2005. *Human Development Report 2005: International Cooperation at a Crossroads*. New York. p 21

[2] Ibid. p. 20

[3] World Bank (1981) *World Development Report 1980*. Washingon DC, World Bank

[4] INTRAC (1998): *Direct Funding from a Southern Perspective; Strengthening Civil Society?* Oxford, INTRAC

[5] Alan Fowler (1997): *Striking a balance*. London, Earthscan

[6] Lester Munson and Phillip Christenson (1996): 'Review of USAID Program in South Africa', 5 November 1996; cited in Nelson Mandela (1997): 'Reports by the President of the ANC, Nelson Mandela, to the 50th National Conference of the African National Congress', Mafikeng, 16 December 1997.

AFTERWORD

Return me to my ordinary humanity, so that you don't commit the intolerable penance of bending over backwards trying to compensate for all the stuff one suffers in silence.

— **Ben Okri,** *In Arcadia*[1]

On New Year's Day 2008, a church building that was sheltering displaced people near the town of Eldoret in Kenya's Rift Valley province was burned by a mob. Within hours, the international media was describing the incident as yet another case of ethnic cleansing in Africa. Images of a victim's charred wheelchair – the only thing that survived the fire – were broadcast worldwide. Kenya, said the foreign correspondents, was descending into a Rwanda-like genocide. The authoritative *Economist* magazine even claimed that whole towns in the western part of the country had been ethnically cleansed, as did many other sections of the Western media.[2] By the first week of February, more than 1,200 people had been killed and some 300,000 were internally displaced.

The post-election violence that rocked Kenya in the first two months of 2008 ignited the imagination of all those who claim to know and love Africa. The world rallied around Kenya in order to save it from itself. United Nations Secretary-General Ban Ki-Moon paid a visit to Kenya during those horror-filled weeks, as did U.S. Secretary of State Condoleezza Rice and Nobel Laureate Desmond Tutu. In an unusual show of solidarity, the African Union sent their envoy, Kofi Annan, to mediate peace talks between the two warring parties – Mwai

Kibaki's Party of National Unity, which was accused of rigging the December 2007 elections, and Raila Odinga's Orange Democratic Movement, which believed its presidential candidate had been robbed of victory.

Meanwhile, there was a flurry of behind-the-scenes activity among Western diplomats who lobbied to force the two parties to sign a peace deal. After some arm-twisting, especially by the U.S. government (which threatened to explore "a wide range of options" if no deal was struck), an agreement to form a Grand Coalition Government was signed on 28 February 2008. Had it not been for the intense pressure exerted by the United States and the European Union, not to mention NGOs, spontaneous civil society movements and the African Union itself, Kenya may have descended into the abyss known as "The Failed African State". Rice's visit – a short stopover during President George Bush's five-nation Africa tour in February 2008 – was a clear indication that Kenyans would suffer if they did not tow the U.S. line. Rumours of sanctions against Kenya by Western governments became rife, as did speculation about whether the U.S. government would strike Kenya as it did Iraq some five years earlier. U.S. military strategists probably wondered if the country's collapse would unleash revolutionary or Al Qaeda-type terrorists in Eastern Africa and the Horn, thereby severely hampering the U.S.-led war on terror. Kenya is also important to the East Africa region: the Kenyan port of Mombasa serves as a crucial transport link for seven land-locked neighbouring countries. A collapsing Kenya could take down several countries with it.

Meanwhile, as Kenya burned, George Bush was on his Africa "Compassion" tour (which did not include a visit to Kenya but which took place when the mayhem in Kenya was at its peak). The musician and self-styled "saviour of Africa", Bob Geldof, who was part of the presidential entourage, praised the U.S. president for having "saved millions upon millions of lives and healed broken bodies" through his campaign to provide free antiretroviral drugs to HIV/Aids patients.

Why, apart from the moral imperative, was it important that Africans stay healthy and alive? Geldof provided some answers:

Africa is the only continent yet to be built. It will be here that some of the great politics of our century will play themselves out. It's a continent of 900 million potential producers and consumers. There are more languages and cultural diversity in Africa than almost anywhere else. Many of the great rivers and resources on the planet are here.

The Chinese and the Indians are massive investors in Africa, and so must the West be. The U.S. gets 19 per cent of its oil imports from the continent, and the figure is rising; in China, it's 30 per cent and rising. Europe must look more to Africa to avoid Russian oil. Europe is a mere 8 miles (13 km) north of this vast continent, with all the tensions over security and immigration that implies.[3]

The long-term implications of Western intervention during the Kenyan crisis may not yet be felt, but should be a cause for worry. In an online discussion a few weeks after the Grand Coalition was formed, Kenyatta University lecturer Godwin Murunga wrote that the main reason for foreign intervention in Kenya was because "Kenyans threatened to destroy the very edifice that supports comprador parasitism and foreign exploitation":

Foreigners resorted to a grand coalition that was so quickly cobbled together, they had no time to anticipate protocol problems. In Nigeria, where there was no popular uprising and where the elections were so thoroughly rigged, *kondoo na mchele* (Condi Rice), as a comedian put it, never showed up. In Zimbabwe, where foreigners seem to have nothing to lose at the moment, they have not mounted similar pressure on Comrade Bob...Foreign intervention [in Kenya] was a reaction to an assertion of popular autonomous action. Foreigners shudder at the fact of such a popular uprising...They will never let it go that bad again.[4]

Indeed, as John Githongo, the exiled anti-corruption chief who unmasked several cases of graft during Kibaki's first presidential term, has stated, the upside of the Kenyan crisis was that it empowered the region and the African Union to demonstrate that they can intervene robustly when things start to go terribly wrong in an African country. The downside was that "the giant sucking sound when the Annan deal was signed was Kenya's sovereignty being flushed into the global diplomatic ether".[5]

Within days of the signing of the peace deal, Kibaki, Odinga and other members of the new coalition government met with key donors to seek financial assistance for "the rebuilding of Kenya". Donors happily obliged, because they know, as this book tries to show, that a donor-dependant country is easier to control. The only section of Kenyan society that did not appear too pleased with this scenario was the non-governmental sector. During the crisis, many of the more than 3,500 registered NGOs in the country had frantically drawn up proposals to attract funding from donors for peace-building activities. Several other "briefcase NGOs" had sprung up out of the blue to take advantage of the situation. NGOs thrive in crises, and the crisis in Kenya was seen by many as an opportunity to build nest eggs that could see them through the lean times. A peace deal could put a brake on these efforts.

In several strife-torn African countries, NGOs are known to run parallel governments of sorts, with their own airstrips and gated communities. Mohamed Osman, a consular at the Somalia embassy in Nairobi, is quoted to have said that Somalia continues to bleed partly because NGOs in the war-torn country are fomenting trouble so that the donor dollar can continue flowing. While a handful of NGOs provide genuine humanitarian relief, noted Kenya's *Standard* newspaper, "many are suspected to create an artificial crisis or to collude in such activities so as to justify their existence."[6]

What Kenya lost during those violence-filled days in 2008 was more than just its sovereignty; it lost its moral high ground in the international community. Never again can a Kenyan diplomat make a case for self-sufficiency or independence in matters affecting the continent. Kenya, once the least donor-dependant country in Eastern Africa, now has no choice but to succumb to donor pressure. This loss will be borne by present and future generations of Kenyans for years to come.

With some luck, the new coalition government will wisen up and seek ways to restore normalcy and bring about fundamental reforms to the country without mortgaging the country's soul.

Rasna Warah
Nairobi, March 2008

Notes

1 Okri, Ben (2002), *In Arcadia*, Phoenix House, an imprint of Orion Books, London.
2 "Ethnic Cleansing in Luoland" (2008) *Economist*, 9 February.
3 Geldof, Bob (2008) "The Healer", *TIME*, 3 March.
4 Submitted to kenyanwriters@googlegroups.com in April 2008.
5 Githongo, John (2008), "From the Ground Up", *TIME*, March 17.
6 "NGOs Thrive in Political Crisis", *The Standard*, 12 March 2008.

ABOUT THE AUTHORS

Sunny Bindra

Sunny Bindra is a management consultant, writer and teacher based in Nairobi, Kenya. He specialises in corporate strategy and governance, and works as an advisor to leading corporations. He also writes a popular and irreverent column "A Sunny Day" in the *Sunday Nation*, East Africa's highest-circulation newspaper.

Parselelo Kantai

Parselelo Kantai is Kenyan writer and journalist who has been published in various journals, newspapers and magazines, including *The Times Literary Supplement*, *The Financial Times* and *The Journal of East African Studies*. He also contributes to *The Sunday Times (South Africa)*. In Nairobi, he co-edited *Ecoforum*, an environmental magazine, and is a former editor of *Executive*, Kenya's oldest business monthly, now defunct. He has been a Chevening scholar at Birkbeck College, London and a Reuters Fellow at Oxford University. In 2004 he began to write fiction. His debut short story *Comrade Lemma and the Black Jerusalem Boys Band* was published in *Kwani?*, a Kenyan literary journal, and was shortlisted for the Caine Prize for African Literature. He is currently working on his first novel.

Isisaeli Kazado

Isisaeli Kazado has worked as a development consultant and practitioner for more than 17 years. Now semi-retired, she spends much of her time tending to other more important matters, such as gardening and reading.

Firoze Manji

Firoze Manji, a former director of Amnesty International's Africa Programme, is the founder and director of Fahamu, a non-governmental organisation with bases in Kenya, Senegal, South Africa and Oxford, U.K. He is also the editor of *Pambazuka News*, an online journal devoted to issues concerning social justice in Africa.

Maina Mwangi
Maina Mwangi is a Kenyan investment banker who is currently based in Lagos, Nigeria.

Bantu Mwaura
Bantu Mwaua is an award-winning performing artist, director, playwright, poet and storyteller from Kenya. His poetry has been published in several collections and anthologies, and his plays have been performed in Kenya, Zimbabwe, the USA, and the UK. Bantu undertook his PhD studies at the New York University's Performance Studies Department. His research work has largely focused on examining how performance theory interfaces with theatre practice in Africa and on the politics of the performance space specifically in Kenya. He is also the founding editor of *Jahazi*, a journal on the arts, culture and performance.

Philip Ochieng
Philip Ochieng, a veteran Kenyan journalist and columnist, is co-author of *The Kenyatta Succession* (1980) and author of *I Accuse the Press: An Insider"s View of the Media and Politics in Africa* (1992).

Onyango Oloo
Onyango Oloo is a Kenyan social justice activist, political commentator and community development consultant. A former political prisoner, Oloo spent close to twenty years in Canada where he worked with a variety of non-profit organizations in addition to being a radio programmer for over fifteen years with community radio stations in Toronto and Montreal. He was also the National Coordinator of the Kenya Social Forum, which was part of the World Social Forum Nairobi 2007 Secretariat.

Lara Pawson
Lara Pawson was born and bred in London, U.K. She is a freelance journalist who has worked in several African countries for over a decade. She has lived in Angola, Ivory Coast, Ghana, South African and Mali and travelled to

many other places. The bulk of her work has been with the BBC World Service but she has also written for *The Independent*, *The Irish Times*, *The Guardian*, *Radical Philosophy*, Reuters, Associated Press, *New Statesman*, *African Business*, *New African Magazine*, *Africa Analysis*, *The Economist* among others. In June 2007, her strong critique of British journalism's response to Africa was published in a book, *Communicating War: Memory, Media, Military*, from Cambridge Scholars' Press. A frustrated and tormented reporter, she also lets loose on her blog www.unstrung-larapawson.blogspot.com, and is currently working on a book about Angola. Her desire is to slowly slide out of the media world and into the art world of fiction and books.

Achal Prabhala
Achal Prabhala is a writer and researcher based in Bangalore, India.

Victoria Schlesinger
Victoria Schlesinger is a science and environmental journalist living in New York City. She has published in *Harper's* magazine, *Discover* magazine and *Scientific American online*, reports for PBS Frontline, and is author of *Animals and Plants of the Ancient Maya*, University of Texas Press. www.vschlesinger.com.

Kalundi Serumaga
Kalundi Serumaga is a Ugandan film producer who was once a refugee in Kenya. He has spent many years as a community activist and as a media columnist and radio talk show host in Uganda. His ancestral burial grounds were part of the land that was recently taken over by a large-scale palm oil plantation on the Ssese Islands.

Issa G. Shivji
Prof. Issa G. Shivji was, until his recent retirement, Professor of Law at the University of Dar es Salaam, where he taught for more than 35 years. He has authored over a dozen books and numerous articles. His books

include *Class Struggles in Tanzania* (1976), *The Concept of Human Rights in Africa* (1989) and *Not Yet Democracy: Reforming Land Tenure in Tanzania* (1998).

Binyavanga Wainaina

Binyavanga Wainaina is the founder and editor of *Kwani?*, the first significant literary magazine to come out of East Africa since *Transition*. He was born in 1971 in Nakuru, Kenya and attended Mangu High School and Lenana School before studying commerce at the University of Transkei. He then moved to Cape Town, South Africa, where he worked for some years as a freelance food and travel writer. In July 2002 he won the Caine Prize for African Writing for his short story "Discovering Home". He is currently writing a book based on this short story for *Granta* and is working on his first novel, *The Fallen World of Appearances*.

Rasna Warah

Rasna Warah has been variously described as a "slum journalist" and a "failed novelist". She has worked as an editor for the United Nations Human Settlements Programme (UN-HABITAT) and is a respected columnist with Kenya's *Daily Nation* newspaper. She is also the author of a book entitled *Triple Heritage (1998)*, which explores the social, economic and political history of Asians in Kenya. Her articles and essays have been published in various national and international newspapers and magazines, including South Africa's *Mail and Guardian*, the *East African* and *Kwani?*

Printed in the United States
133623LV00001B/8/P

9 781434 386038